Can You Smell the Rain?

Can You Smell the Rain?

poems

Patricia Cleary Miller

Foreword by H. L. Hix

BkMk Press
University of Missouri-Kansas City

BkMk Press
University of Missouri-Kansas City
5101 Rockhill Road
Kansas City, Missouri 64110
www.umkc.edu/bkmk

Executive Editor: Robert Stewart
Managing Editor: Ben Furnish
Assistant Managing Editor: Cynthia Beard

Author photo: Lifetouch
Cover photo: Cynthia Beard

BkMk Press wishes to thank Kelsey Beck, Sarah Chapman, Harmony Lassen, and Henry Shi. Special thanks to Gayle Levy.

Missouri
Arts Council
The State of the Arts

Financial assitance for this project has been provided by the Missouri Arts Council, a state agency.

ISBN 978-1-943491-21-6

Library of Congress Cataloging-in-Publication Data

Names: Miller, Patricia Cleary, author. | Hix, H. L., writer of foreword.
Title: Can you smell the rain? : poems / Patricia Cleary Miller ; foreword
   by H.L. Hix.
Description: Kansas City, Missouri : BkMk Press, University of
   Missouri-Kansas City, [2020] | Summary: "Most of the poems in this
   collection, set largely in Kansas City, Missouri, deal with women's
   perspectives on coming of age, love, family, as well as the nature of
   artistic transcendence, reflecting subjects across several decades in
   the 20th and 21st centuries"-- Provided by publisher.
Identifiers: LCCN 2020002380 | ISBN 9781943491216 (paperback)
Subjects: LCSH: Women--Poetry | LCGFT: Poetry.
Classification: LCC PS3563.I4194 C36 2020 | DDC 811/.54--dc23
LC record available at https://lccn.loc.gov/2020002380

This book is set in ITC Leawood Std.

for Sappho, who started it all

Acknowledgments

Rockhurst Review: "Summer Dancing," "Philomel, Postulant," "The Blue Neon Word," "Portovenere," "Millefiori," "I Could Have Taken the Other Bridge," "Mother Is Scrubbing Her Floors," "Mother Remembers Flowers," "For Yvette Chauviré," "My Burberry Raincoat," and "One Single Blueberry"

I-70 Review: "The Big Nun," "Paris Dress," and "Too Brilliant"

The Same: "Daddy Said," and "She Waits"

Publications of the Missouri Philological Association: "Irises in the Tribal Grill"

Thorny Locust: "Except For"

Spud Songs: "Mollie O'Rourke Cleary Explains"

Kansas City Outloud II: 32 Contemporary Area Poets:

New Letters: "Mother Won't Wear Walking Shoes"

Crimson Lights: "Mother Won't Wear Walking Shoes," "Mollie O'Rourke Cleary Explains," and "Menaced by Flowers"

The Shining Years, edited by Gary Lechliter: "Mother Is Dying"

Stand: "The John Harvard Charm Bracelet" and "When a First Time?"

Big Muddy: "Black Jack"

Many wise and kind people have encouraged and inspired my writing, have read and edited and published my work, have told me stories. Without them I could not have written these poems and this book would not exist. Charles Kovich, Dan Martin, Rita Shelton, James Engell, Charles Egan, Bill Schwartz, Peggy and John Heywood have read and critiqued my drafts. Maryfrances Wagner, Greg Field, Gloria Vando, Robert Stewart, Sylvia Kofler, Phil and Nancy Miller have published my poems. The Diversifiers make me produce. Notre Dame de Sion, Radcliffe College, Harvard University, Cynthia Siebert, my Rockhurst University students, and the Kelton, Cleary and Miller families give me topics. And Ben Furnish and Cynthia Beard have produced this book. Thank you all, much more than I can say.

Contents

9   Foreword by H. L. Hix

I.

13   Mère Ida

14   Mollie O'Rourke Cleary Explains

15   Where the Kaw Angles Fast into the Missouri River

16   You Are Such Good Children

21   Little Boys

28   The Big Nun

33   History of My Hair

35   We All Like Shiny Boots

37   Summer Dancing

39   The John Harvard Charm Bracelet

41   Philomel, Postulant

43   How Long?

44   The Blue Neon Word

45   Too Brilliant

46   Portovenere

50   Millefiori

52   When a First Time?

53   Except For

54   Black Glass Beads

56   Prunella

57   The Protectors

58   I Am Always Holding a Baby

59   Emily Is Sitting

60   I Could Have Taken the Other Bridge

II.

65   She Waits

66   Toronto

68   Waiting All My Life

70   Mother Is Scrubbing Her Floors

71   Who Will Hold Me?

73   Mother Mourns

74   Portuguese Motets

76   Mother Remembers Flowers

78   To the Virgin in Saint-Sulpice

80   Veni Creator

81   Daddy Said

83   Black Jack

87   Mother Won't Wear Walking Shoes

88   Mother Won't Buy Polypropylene

89   Elva Remembered

92   Mother Is Dying

93   For Yvette Chauviré (1917–2016)

95   Chinese Box of Love Scenes

97   After Reading about Chinese Foot-binding

98   The Bride

99   My Burberry Raincoat

102   Menaced by Flowers

103   Irises in the Tribal Grill

104   Lace

105   Katherine Dunham: on Haitian Dance

106   One Single Blueberry

107   Une Seule Myrtille

110   The Alarm Clock

111   Only His Bones Remain

112   When Sylvia Heard Her Orpheus Singing

Foreword

William Carlos Williams was onto something with his aphorism, "No ideas but in things," but Patricia Cleary Miller's *Can You Smell the Rain?* goes Williams one better. Miller doesn't have to say what her poems prove: No moments but in things, no memories, no lives, no loves. These are poems (or, I would say, this is a lyric memoir) lush with vivid and vivifying particulars: "calico envelopes, rick-rack trimmed"; "pastel-colored rosaries that glow in the dark"; "squirt guns and candy cigarettes and / little metal mice that clicked like crickets"; the fender of a silver motorcycle with sunlight glancing off it, a tablecloth of brown and blue batik, pearl-headed pins in an embroidered pincushion. These are (in all the ways one might mean the phrase) the objects of a lifetime, and they impress themselves on the reader as they have on the poet. At one point, Miller recalls from school assembly the metal folding chairs whose seats have patterned perforations that "make little bubbles on your fingertips / if you sit on your hands": her poems, like those patterned perforations, leave their mark.

—H. L. Hix

I

Mère Ida

Viens ici, ma petite chérie,
the old round-faced nun, so big, whispers to me
from behind her huge desk on its high platform.
I stand up beside my little desk.

Viens ici, she repeats.
I stand stiffly beside my little desk.

Viens ici, Patricia. Approche, she hisses at me.
I tremble beside my little desk.

My classmates stare at me,
they laugh. No one says a word.

Mère Ida's face reddens, she clenches her fists.
I shudder. I stand stiffly beside my little desk.
I start to cry.

Nine years old, my first day
at Notre Dame de Sion, French Convent school,
the only person who does not understand a word of French.
I sob. Mère Ida grumbles. The students laugh.

⚬

In Parisian French Mère Ida had crooned,
Come here, my little darling.
She expected to love me as she had loved Daddy
when he was small. But she always scared me.
She preferred the *enfants espiègles,* the naughty lively ones,
as Daddy must have been.

I think that I had flunked third grade—
we moved from Long Island to Saint Davids
to Kansas City. At Swinney School,
far behind grade level, I loved all the darling boys.
I think my parents and grandparents conspired—
they hoped the French Convent,
now an all-girls school, would reform me.

Mollie O'Rourke Cleary Explains

We were aristocrats in Clare,
Tipperary, Killarney, Kildare.
We garnished our baked potatoes
with bitter Spanish marmalade.
In French boarding schools we studied
literature and embroidery.
I'm sure we had castles and gardens
and forests, and we rode to the hounds.

I'm sure that Patrick, my papa,
came over here for adventure,
and Catherine, my mama, got bored
in Killarney and ran off with
her nanny, whose beau had sailed away
for St. Louis, where Patrick, with
his bright sapphire eyes and black moustache,
though as old as her father, steamed

Catherine up the wide Missouri
to the town of the Kanza, the land
of the People of the South Wind.
They watched the first bridge, for the first
railroad and started Delmonico
Hotel and built the huge stone house
on new Linwood Boulevard, and then

Mama and I dressed like sisters
in white lace gowns and wide feathered
hats, and cook made *pommes frites* and new
American scalloped potatoes,
and we all spoke French. But they never
told Irish stories, though we were
always aristocrats, I'm sure.

Where the Kaw Angles Fast into the Missouri River

After They Built the Bridge
Patrick O'Rourke steamed up this river to Delmonico Hotel,
waited tables, tended bar, bought that hotel
and its land and more land and built a huge granite house.
His daughter wore white lace gowns.
His granddaughter drinks at Knuckleheads
by the train tracks as the tattooed bikers jam.
His great granddaughter sat on the ASB Bridge
contemplating, her dead baby inside her.

On the Floodplain
They changed the law:
we can't recycle our wine bottles anymore.
We can buy a dented refrigerator,
sell our old curtain rods, admire ancient cars—
yard art—dance with tattooed Tiffany.
One day together we will climb
the bluffs, explore the floodplain—
find rattlesnakes
and Lewis and Clark's flat stone outcropping,
hear paddleboats, then steamboats, drop merchandise
to birth Kansas City.

Before the City Was
Before Sacagawea, even, were the grasses,
bison, eagles, perhaps an ivory-billed woodpecker.
Now a blues bar, rusted streets, tottering brick warehouses.
Perhaps tattooed Tiffany will sing to me of waving grasses.

You Are Such Good Children: Four Memory Poems

(At Notre Dame de Sion, French Convent in Kansas City, 1948-1957)

I. Prendre Sa Note: Self Scrutiny
The *Maîtresse de Classe* strides into the classroom,
her fifteen-decade rosary, all the mysteries—
the beads are olive pits from the Mount of Olives—
rattling softly, she turns toward us, looking stern.
Stand up quietly, do not let your chair
scrape the shiny hardwood floor, do not
make a sound. Take one step to the right,
hold your pleated skirt out slightly,
curtsy, say Bonjour, ma Mère.
The *Maîtresse de Classe*—Mère Joselina, Mère Ida,
Mère Alphonsina, Mère Clarella—
bows back at us, smiles, *Bonjour, mes enfants.*

Her shiny black Cuban-heeled oxfords clicking,
she swirls up the two steps of her big square
oak platform, sits down at her desk,
perches on the very front edge of her chair,
never leaning back, her spine rigid but relaxed.
She takes up her grade book and her pen,
unscrews the top of her ink bottle,
uncaps her pen, and dips the tip into the ink bottle.
Step back to the left, sit down. Soundlessly.

Every morning, each child, in alphabetical order:
stand up at your desk, grade yourself.
A scale of one to ten, on four actions:
Ordre, Application, Politesse, Règlements—
Orderliness, Studies, Courtesy, Rules.
Prendre sa Note—*Taking note,*
examining one's conscience.
The *Maîtresse de Classe* marks each *note* in her gradebook.
If, very rarely, you give yourself a ten in each area,
the *Maîtresse de Classe* says you have a *Note d'Honneur.*
You strive each day. The points accumulate.

II. Bons Points

Our desks have slanted tops on hinges,
a hole on the top flat part for the ink bottle.
Inside, books and notebooks in precise piles
and three calico envelopes, rick-rack trimmed.

In one is *le voile,* small black lace veil, for chapel.
In the second, scraps of dark cloth, pen wipes—
Never ever wipe ink on your skirt, which is
navy blue, precisely pressed and pleated.
The pens leak on our fingers.
In the third envelope we collect our *bons points,*
small squares of bright construction paper
stamped with black numbers—5, 10, 15, 20.

The *Maîtresse de Classe* assigns chores:
straighten the desks neatly;
erase the blackboard quickly;
help another pupil with penmanship or embroidery;
water the plant (a prehensile Boston fern
that turns brown if you brush against it,
and everyone knows it is you);
turn the lights on or off as instructed—
but don't flicker them or they will burn out
and everyone will know it is you.

The *Maîtresse de Classe* clasps her hands,
sucks in her breath,
pushes out the words:
Ah . . ., you are such good children,
and God loves you very much.
She passes out these *bons points.*
We never figure out the system—
no master list matching chores and points,
yet *bons points* pile up in our calico envelopes.

Now and then, in a pattern we cannot see,
on some saint's feast day—
Cosmas and Damian, Hilarion, Polycarp—
a table loaded with prizes appears
in the front of the classroom:
holy cards encircled with crochet stitching,
gray felt mice with bright glass eyes,
little statues of Mary in her long blue veil,
tiny prayer books etched in gold,
pastel-colored rosaries that glow in the dark;
and always candy—hard lemon drops,
spicy Neccos in rainbow colors,
ugly black licorice that stains our fingers and lips,
Chiclets square like our new front teeth.

Spring and fall we crimp crêpe paper streamers
into ruffles, festoon them along the gym walls
for Mission Day, to rescue pagan babies.
At booths set up in the gym we buy more prizes
with our stash of *bons points.*

These treasures we take to our bedrooms
to set up our own little bedside altars,
to store at last in a special box
under our beds forever.

III. Class Colors, Décorations
Each class has colors: green and white for fourth grade,
solid green for fifth, blue and white for sixth,
solid blue for seventh, on and on: rainbow for tenth
purple and white for eleventh, solid purple for seniors.

Wool decorations for every day, silk for assembly
and big feast days, like May Day.
Everyone has a belt and a neck pendant for a cross—
bone for everyday, nacre for formal days,
with white uniforms—silk blouse, long pleated wool skirt.
First thing each morning, put on your decorations.
At day's end, fold them away neatly in your desk.

Should you misbehave very badly,
take off your cross and give it to the teacher.
Punishment lasts for minutes or hours;
all the school knows of your disgrace.
It almost never happens, but you see
the justice, relish the attention.

For ordinary misbehavior, like laughing,
you stand in the hallway outside the classroom door
for five minutes. Once I was standing there
when Mother walked by on the way to a meeting—
then I was in more trouble, for more laughing.
Worst laughter was when we shot
the handsome young Jesuit chaplain
from black water pistols
with Chanel Nº5 cologne.
He barked and did not laugh,
but the nuns laughed stealthily.

IV. Grande Assemblée
Each month, all teachers and students—
kindergarten to seniors—
white uniforms, long white veils,
shiny black shoes replace ugly brown oxfords—
file silently into *La Grande Salle.*

Folding metal chairs in rows, rubber-tipped feet
quiet on the terrazzo floor, mirror bright.
Patterned perforations on the seats
can make little bubbles on your fingertips
if you sit on your hands.

On the stage, all the teaching nuns, trying to look stern,
nodding approval as each *Maîtresse de Classe*
calls up her own students:
my first class was fourth grade—*Classe Théodore, Classe Verte,*
Théodore Ratisbonne, co-founder of Notre Dame de Sion worldwide.

File up to the front of La Grande Salle,
form a semi-circle facing the stage,
curtsy solemnly, in unison.

All the accumulated daily *Notes*—
now big rewards for schoolwork, for deportment.
Medals for solid courses, tricolor ribbons for French,
cordons, in the color of each class.
From eighth grade on, at the end of each year,
you get to keep your medals.

Many feast days, many prizes;
many assemblies, many ribbons and medals.
The system of rewards—so elaborate and fascinating—
leaves little time for misbehavior and punishment.

Little Boys

I. Kansas City. Three Years Old
Across Pierce Street the boys run run run,
climb over rock walls,
shinny up tree trunks,
hang by their knees from low branches,
make guns out of sticks,
make forts under spirea bushes,
don't have to go inside to go potty,
never get their socks wet.

Mother falls asleep during my nap—
I can cross Pierce Street. I can run run run.

II. Dos Palos, California, Army Base. Three and a Half
My baby sister is sick. Mother never sleeps.
Mother says the barracks is filthy and dark.
The flowered rug makes the dirt floor soft.
Mother walks back and forth across the rug,
singing to the baby. I sneak outside.

The sun shines and the sands move all day.
Concrete pipes so big that all the children
can run through them standing up.
You kids get out of here, the workmen yell.
The ground is shifty, sandy; we run around
through the pipes, they slide down new hills.
We always come out in another place.
You kids get out of here,
the workmen shout, but we can still hide.

III. Los Banos, Little House
Baby throws up, and Mother cries all the time.
When she sees a rat, Daddy moves us to a little house.
There are no boys around, but I have a friend
no one can see, called Hit-a-ma-Hee.
He peers in the dining room window, and

Daddy jumps up from the table and chases him
around the yard but never sees him.

In the front yard is a honeysuckle hedge.
In the back beyond the barbed wire fence
cows stroll by in a little ditch.
I lean over to pat the cows.
I slip on the mud and scratch my arm
and it bleeds, and I get a grass stain on my dress.

Mother shoves Baby to Mary Pereira
and finds a car and rushes me to the hospital
for a shot. Later she dabs milk on my dress
and the grass stain comes out.

   4. Saint Davids, Pennsylvania, at Granny and Grandpa's. Four
After that Daddy puts us all on a train.
We ride across the whole country to Philadelphia.
The train is full of soldiers. I am their girlfriend.
I sit on their laps, and they read to me.
Mother takes care of baby Cathy;
she is still sick and always crying.
We stop in Kansas City in the middle of the night;
Mama and Papa Cleary get on the train for a minute.
They give me a doll with a blue silk dress.

In Philadelphia Granny and Grandpa Kelton
meet us at the train. Mother faints.
Granny cannot get her pulse,
and Mother has to sleep for a week.
Granny takes care of baby Cathy.

Granny has a magnolia tree to climb
and spirea bushes to hide in,
and on her block are a lot of children,
and I learn to pee outside and not get my socks wet.

5. Saint Davids, Kindergarten
The boys sing "Pop Goes the Weasel" with a new word
I do not know. They sing it over and over
and laugh and laugh and dance all around
the classroom. They knock over the houses we made
of huge cardboard blocks, big boxes of cardboard
painted to look like bricks. The teachers scream
and chase the boys, boxy bricks flying.
The teachers shout and catch the boys and box
their ears and wash their mouths out with soap
and make them sit in the cloakroom. We laugh and laugh.

I try to remember the bad word. I want to sing
it at home and make a ruckus. That will be easy
because Grandpa yells a lot. When he gets home
at night he goes down to the basement and makes a racket.
I like the smells of sawdust and plexiglass,
of turpentine and glue. I think Uncle
Stanton invented plexiglass. I play
with the samples in all colors of a dark rainbow.
I hold them up to the light, and I steal matches
from above the stove and try to set the little
squares on fire because I like the smell.

I eat early in the kitchen before Grandpa gets home.
I am supposed to greet him, then go upstairs to bed.
Mother is already upstairs with Cathy.

To get Grandpa to come to dinner Granny yells
down the basement stairs, but the power tools
make too much noise. Then Granny flicks off the light,
and the tools stop. Then Grandpa yells words I do know.
I like to hear Grandpa yell. Granny doesn't.

This particular night, as usual, Mother
and Granny and Grandpa are in the dining room,

23

Cathy is playing upstairs in her crib, and I
am supposed to be reading in my room. However, I sneak
down the front stairs and start dancing around in the front hall.
I sing the little song from school. The grown-ups
keep eating and chatting. I sing louder. Nothing.
Again: *All around the [nevermind] tree,*
the monkey chased the weasel. Finally:
Grandpa rushes out of the dining room,
brandishing a silver salad fork, yelling
words I understand. I sing louder
and faster and dash up the stairs laughing and laughing.

Thirty years later, Uncle Stanton asks me,
did Grandpa hurt me, was I afraid of him?

Imagine Grandpa: managing defense contracts
at his chemical plant, but required to prove loyalty
because the founders were German.
Head of a complex household in wartime.
A frail toddler and her frantic mother.
His teenaged son annoying the neighbors by blasting
his trombone out the attic dormer.
His medical-student son letting researchers
do chemical warfare experiments on his leg.
His glamorous younger daughter shipping off
with the USO to Japan to find her boyfriend.
His grandiose mother visiting from Ohio
where she refused to pay her bills and hid
her cash irretrievably in her thousands of rare books.
His patient opera-trained wife, cooking lunch
for "hoboes" after they weeded the Victory Garden,
and driving an ambulance during air-raids—
German U-boats along the shore, all villages blacked out—
while the naughty toddler snatches her aunt's
manicure scissors to cut star-shaped
patterns in the blackout shades.

And a little rascal of a kindergartener.
All he wanted was a peaceful dinner.

How could I be afraid of him? Every
morning I sat on his bed while he coughed through
his first cigarette and showed me his butterflies and rocks
all catalogued on green shelves up to the ceiling.

Daddy was away in the War,
so Grandpa was the first father to all my dolls.
He showed me the Empire State Building,
the Cathedral of Saint John the Divine, being built.
He bought me a tiny bronze mountain goat
at the Museum of Natural History.
He gave me a postcard of Fra Filippo Lippi,
"La Virgine che adora il Bambino."
It is still on my dresser after all these years.

6. *Third Grade Adventures*
At Saint Boniface School in Sea Cliff, Long Island,
sixty-four children, our desks in long rows,
mine was by the windows. We were quiet.
Sister Stephanie was quiet and pretty.
Then she got sick, and we could not visit her,
and she never came back.

At Christmas, Mother and Cathy took the train
to Saint Davids. I went with Daddy in the car.
In the Blizzard of '47 we drove through New York
through Philadelphia to Saint Davids.
The snow was swirling and the streets were deserted,
and we drove all night through whirling foggy snow.
Huge flakes falling slowly. Streetlights in the fog.

All winter we stayed at Granny and Grandpa's.
Mother's old teachers came to the house:
Miss Usher for arithmetic, Miss McDevitt for reading.

They were sweet and smiley,
but I just wanted to build forts in the snow.

When we got to Kansas City it was light all day.
I got the measles and a new radio and had
to stay in bed with my eyes closed.
I listened every day to *The Romance
of Helen Trent* and *Our Gal Sunday*.

When I finally went to school I had forgotten everything
Miss Usher and Miss McDevitt had taught me,
but I liked walking with Cathy up the long hill to Swinney School,
and I liked the big noisy classroom with boys.
The desks were not in rows, they were all over
the place and we played and sang in the classroom.
We sang "Home on the Range" and "Don't Fence Me In."
I learned all the words. If we had books,
I never opened them. All the boys were tall and strong,
and they made a lot of noise and ran around on the playground.
I could only watch them because the girls played separately.

When I turned nine Mother said we would go
on a picnic to Swope Park, and I could invite nine guests.
I chose nine boys. I remember their names:
Danny Sipes, Russell Wallace, Fred Farris . . .

Mother tried briefly, but soon gave up dissuasion.
Daddy got a stopwatch and a clothesline.
Mother made deviled eggs and potato salad.
She wore a crisp green-striped sundress.
Mama Cleary wore a long purple dress
and brought a pink and blue quilt.
I don't remember my dress, but I know
that none of the boys commented on it.
We three ladies sat calmly on the quilt and smiled.

Daddy taught the boys different kinds of knots
and chased them around and tied them to a tree
and timed their escapes from the rope.

We ladies sang and laughed and ate potato salad
and clapped when the boys escaped from the rope.
Mother gave prizes to everyone:
squirt guns and candy cigarettes and
little metal mice that clicked like crickets.

Mother and Mama said that boys that age
don't like to sit on a quilt in the shade.

The Big Nun

Rambling the Labyrinth with Mère Marthanna

At the French Convent of Notre Dame de Sion everyone spoke French, all the time. We had to learn French if we wanted lunch, the volleyball, a string for the straps of our bathing suits. Then one day appeared Mère Marthanna, speaking English (though her name had the staccato French pronunciation—Mahr-tah-nah).

Part I: First Lessons: The Existence of God

Tall and thin and pale—a long face, big teeth, popping black eyes, no eyebrows.
In Cuban-heeled lace-up oxfords, she glided straight and tall into our eighth-grade classroom, black robes swirling. She stepped up onto the dais.

Good morning, people. I will call you people *because that is what you are. I do not like children, but they told me to teach you, and I am here. Therefore you are not children.*

She stepped down off the dais, her fifteen decade rosary made of olive pits from the Mount of Olives (so we had been told) clicking against the desk's straight wooden legs. She was still tall.

Take out your religion book. Show it to me. As I thought: it is stupid. Put it away.

She swept back onto the platform.

We will begin by learning Saint Thomas Aquinas's five proofs for the existence of God through reason. Saint Thomas is not in your book; we will make our own book.

She gazed at us and then stared out the window.

Look around you. How do you know that God exists?

No one answered. We were frozen in fear. She was so tall. And she was speaking English.
None of the other nuns spoke English. Mère Marthanna spoke English just like our parents.
She did not have an accent at all.

No one answered. Mère Marthanna glared. Then her long bony hands rose slowly from her sides in two giant arcs, as though she were going to fly; as her elbows bent, her index fingers jabbed out, and she bored them right into her concave temples. Her eyes popped.

THINK, she growled. *God gave you a brain. Use it. Now look about the room. Now write where you see God. Five minutes.*

After five minutes she said,

That is all. Bring me your papers tomorrow, neatly written in pen, 500 words.

For some days we tried to make our own proofs for the existence of God, then we moved on to Saint Thomas: we wrote essays, we listed objections, we gave our own interpretations. I still remember the Unmoved Mover, the First Cause, Design, Necessity. And I remember the midterm exam. One question: *Prove the Existence of God from Reason.* We had three days to write our answers, and we turned them in on Friday. On Monday morning, Mère Marthanna strode into class, ascended the dais, the stack of papers in her left hand. We knew we were all getting *A*s.

She rapped the stack with the back of her right hand, then ripped the whole stack in half.
She snarled,
The question asked, Prove the Existence of God from Reason. *Each of you told me what Saint Thomas said. I did not ask what Saint Thomas said. And he is wrong. You cannot prove the existence of God from reason.*

For weeks she had been leading us through a labyrinth.

We did learn Saint Thomas. We learned to question and to observe and to write.

She did not make us retake the exam because we had already written so much, and she knew that we knew.
And after she scared us, she gave us all *As*.

Sometime later, remembering that she had ordered us to *THINK*, we voted that we did not believe in hell, and we marched in a delegation up to Mère Marthanna to inform her of our conviction, expecting, even hoping, that we would get in a lot of trouble, and maybe even be expelled. She just shrugged her shoulders and said *So?* We thought she smiled as she stalked away. We believed that she was pleased.

Like most of the Sisters of Notre Dame de Sion—benevolent, positive, well-educated—Mère Marthanna was witty and brilliant; and she was a trickster. Playing with our developing intellects, she would lead us into forests out of which we could not easily reason our way. That was a heady day when we thought we could outsmart her with our rejection of hell, but we probably just strode into another of her traps.

Part II: Mère Marthanna's Rules
Besides Religion, Mère Marthanna taught Christian Family Living, a theoretical home economics course (without the mundane title) that addressed posture, fashion, home design, and a few recipes. Mère Marthanna told us that salad dressing was simply oil, vinegar, salt, and pepper and that it did not come pre-prepared in a bottle. She gave us her famous recipe for Spanish rice for fifty; this school specialty was served only at festivals and at the monthly Mothers Meetings, never to the students at our daily lunches of mystery meat, gray Le Sueur petite peas, and whitish lettuce drowned in apple cider vinegar—no such thing as extra-virgin olive oil.

We learned that horizontal stripes make you look fat, that an overall color scheme makes you look tall, and that black always looks smart. Sleeveless blouses were taboo because they could cause some pitiful man riding by on a bus to think bad thoughts and later commit an unspeakable crime. We learned that *lines of cleavage* must never show and that we should always dress in a Mary-like way, like God's mother in the larger-than-life statue high above the altar. (We did not know then that in some early Renaissance paintings Mary's nursing breast was bare.) The upper-class boarder from Russell, Kansas, who wore the new pointy bras with circular stitching, did not return after Christmas. We reasoned that she was an "experienced" girl and that our mothers petitioned Notre Mère, the Mother Superior, to send her back to Russell. Or perhaps her own parents found her a husband.

Mère Marthanna taught us posture: to rotate our hips in their sockets so our knees would not knock and our arches would not fall, to pull our shoulder blades in and down so that we would not get humpbacks. And most importantly, *Sion girls sit with their knees pinched together.* As she said this Mère Marhanna would tap all her fingertips together like castanets and would quiver the word *pinched* like a long violin note.

One of Mère Marthanna's extensive exercises was to make us design our dream house, with special attention to all the details of the kitchen: placement of windows, the way the refrigerator door swung open, the number of steps to the stove.

Then she instructed us to redesign the house with no electricity. *How will you live without a refrigerator?* We did not understand her. Did she mean for us to simplify? Not to be greedy? Or was she crazy impractical? I could never answer that question, though I have long pondered it. Was she a pre-hippy? Or a thoughtful modern woman fifty years early, a *green* woman? But now my own kitchen is practical and simple, and I have not reorganized it or even moved a spatula in decades. I consider my carbon footprint.

As the years pass I continue to ponder and defy her rules. I make my own salad dressing fresh, and I have adapted the Spanish rice recipe for a mere twenty people. But I wear horizontal stripes and bright flowered prints (but not together). I cross my legs and slouch. I regret that I never developed enough lines of cleavage to flaunt and then to shock her with.

Besides constantly admonishing us to THINK, Mère Marthanna would order us, *Never compromise with the Truth.* She never gave details, she never defined the Truth. When she was older, wearing civilian clothes, I visited her at the convent. We were both wearing smart white trousers. I apologized (we had never been allowed to wear pants of any kind, our gym suits had pleated skirts covering bloomers, and even now we never wore pants in front of the nuns) and she smiled in recognition of the past. I reminded her of her constant orders about the Truth. She looked puzzled. *Did I say that?* Then she flashed her old trickster smirk. *Well, I guess you shouldn't. If you can ever figure out what the heck the Truth is.* She said, *What the heck.* She sounded Zen: *what is the sound of one hand clapping; if you see the Buddha on the road kill him.* We went out to lunch. The world had moved on too far now for dining in public with a nun, both of you trendily dressed in white trousers, to be a defiant act.

Later I would visit her in retirement and then in the hospital. I did her nails. I sent in my hairdresser. And one day she informed me, *Tomorrow I'm being sent to a nursing home. The French Room is having a sale of cruise wear. I would like some outfits in bright colors—lavender, teal, hot pink, you know what I like.* I brought her four expensive pieces on approval. She stood up, pulled her hospital gown over her head, and stood there naked. I was amazed. She was eighty, but her skin was smooth ivory, with no scars from her mastectomies. She was slender and lovely. She said *I'll try the teal top with the lavender pants first.* She ended up taking all four pieces. As she had told us eighth graders, it's important to look good at all times.

History of My Hair

Granny had wispy fine hair.
So did Mother, who wanted a permanent wave,
the latest thing. Granny said no—wasteful vanity.

So Mother made sure that I always had a tight perm.
She and her friend Lou Anderson convinced me
that my hair was lank, limp, mouse-colored.

Every few months Mother would buy a Toni home perm kit
and haul me off to Lou's apartment
in a colonnaded building on Rockhill Road,
shaded by cathedral elms.
For a few moments we would sit on the breezy porch.
They sipped strong iced tea, I drank orange juice.
They gesticulated long red fingernails
that matched "fire and ice" lipstick.
They smoked Chesterfields—filters not yet thought of—
laughed about their silly husbands. Their hair was tightly curled.

Then they plopped me on a four-legged kitchen stool,
spread newspapers on the rainbow linoleum,
wrapped my hair tightly around hard pink rods,
and painted it with ammonia or embalming fluid—
it smelled like the slimy fetal cats that Sister Irena
was so proud to have procured for biology class—
while I held a graying towel to my eyes, the poison
trickling down my forehead, seeping into the towel.

When I was twelve or thirteen I somehow
got Mother to leave my hair alone.
I think she was pregnant, busy, tired.
I would roll my hair damp on metal rollers,
I trained myself to sleep on them.
We did not have a hair dryer.
I do not think they had been thought of yet.

Still, I followed Mother's rules:
no hair washing after 9 P.M.,
no sleeping on wet hair,
hair washing only on Thursday.

My hair was long and shiny.
Still, for the next few decades, I continued to think
it was fine and wispy. Until my Italian hairdresser,
tall handsome Cesare—black hair, blue eyes—
said my hair was thick, that he could do anything with it.

But now, though still strong, it is geriatric fuzz,
and I depend on top-priced blond Ashley
to blow it dry into perfect poufed luster.

We all Like Shiny Boots

I.
Side by side with empty Chianti bottles,
old tins of shoe polish litter the shore of Libya
in 1942, wherever British troops have been,
Walter Graebner writes to *Time* magazine
from the Tobruk trenches. Ladies like
those shiny boots, disdain rough-shod GIs.
The Brits trade Kiwi tins to Yanks for cigarettes.

II.
On leave from the Pacific, Daddy taught me to shine shoes.
Hard polish brush, hard paste, soft rag, big horsehair buff brush.
Rub and rub in fast circles around and around,
a drop of water; rub and rub, harder, faster.
Buff with the big horsehair brush, back and forth,
back and forth, *da dum*, *da dum*, a heartbeat
rhythm *da dum da dum da dum*, spit polish, mirror shine.
Keep the troops busy, keep their minds off girls. Or death.

III.
In my French boarding school we *had* to wear
brown Oxfords, stylish by rules of some old lady
long ago, or ugly to keep the boys away.
We *had* to keep those shoes shiny.
On fair-weather days, a swipe with a damp cloth
(probably Father's old T-shirt), but most days
full treatment: rub the polish in well, buff hard
with the horsehair brush almost too big for my hand.
Back and forth, hard hard *da dum*, *da dum*, back and forth.
You had to do it hard and fast.
If you did not do it right you would get polish
on your white socks or your leg if, rude and uncivilized,
you rubbed one foot against the other ankle or calf.
And every morning you had to rate your grooming:
polished shoes, ironed blouse, pressed skirt just knee length.

IV.

Yesterday I was tired and dizzy and bored,
missing my Love, needing to accomplish something.
My good boots were white with salt and encrusted with mud.
I scraped and rinsed them in the sink.
I found old rubber gloves and rubbed dried-up Kiwi polish
into those boots, and then two other pairs,
and then a dozen pairs of shoes, and then brushed
back and forth hard hard hard *da dum*, *da du*m
in the rhythm my father taught me,
in the rhythm of the Allied soldiers.
I lined my work up in the hall.
Shined. Waiting.

Summary Dancing

For Robert Lee Poe: 1 April 1936–10 April 2004;
Honour Byrne Waldron: 24 July 1939–23 March 2010

*Frank Lloyd Wright designed Kansas City's Community Christian Church with a
perforated dome through which a spire of light could shine up three miles. One
summer my friends and I painted flats for the church's youth theatre.*

Last night's air was sweet with lilacs.
I sat in the park with my children and grandchildren,
watched fireworks for someone's birthday or wedding.
Explosions of sapphires rubies emeralds topaz diamonds
halfway up to the airplanes, a tower of light
a pedestal for vanishing jewels.

    Can you smell the rain? Faster than light it swirls.
    Can you smell the lilacs? Can you see the fireworks?
    They explode above the steeple of light
    as we ride all summer the barebacked horses
    in the moonlight, in the spring rain.

We girls, launched from Kansas City's French
Convent into the dancing summer, chattered
fluent French, worked to pay for college.

The boys, recruited by a mother as
our prom dates, were older, wiser, already juniors,
with cars and jobs and plans. They never tired.

The eight of us, bored all day in offices,
danced each night—sprinkled Ivory soap flakes
to wax basement floors, driveways under
basketball hoops, Swope Park shelter houses—

sang to music from car radios. The moon
always full, the breeze always cool, never rain.
On plaid blankets we picnicked ham sandwiches,
deviled eggs, chocolate-chip cookies.

Our clothes just ironed. Full skirts, crinolines stiffly
starched, bright Capezio flats. Boys in tan pants,
checked shirts, shiny penny loafers.

At Heywood's father's farm we danced on the porch,
rode barebacked horses by moonlight, fast around
the fields, into the woods, cicadas and tree frogs
chirping. Bob the best rider, best dancer, Fred
Astaire pro, never tired, twirled fast, led so smoothly
I never tripped. We sang *Oh Honeycomb, won't cha
be mah Baby? Oh Honeycomb be mah own.*

> Can you smell the rain? Faster than light
> it twirls. Can you smell the lilacs? Can
> you see the fireworks? They explode above the tower
> of light. Honour and Bob, you now gallop moonlit
> through lilacs, in spring rain, beyond the column of light.

The John Harvard Charm Bracelet

Matt was tall with thick black hair,
eyes green, lashes curled up.
We would chat after Greek poetry class.
My repartee witty, my skirts short.
I think he kissed me once or twice.
Yes, he kissed me once or twice.

At Thanksgiving he took me to a debutante ball;
he escorted another girl, Ellen,
said he still loved his high school crush, Anne.
His father looked after me all evening.

So I was the third. No matter, for his eyes
were green and his lashes curled up,
and he was tall with curly black hair.

In rustling lavender taffeta, my high school prom dress—
tulip skirt, sedately dipping bodice,
sewed by Mother from a Givenchy design—
I was all Paris.

I danced with Matt's father, never met the deb.
Silly Matt in white tie. His eyes were green
and his lashes curled up, and I
was all Paris in rustling lavender taffeta.

At Christmas Matt gave me a bracelet.
Its chain bright gold,
its John Harvard charm dark red.
I think he kissed me once or twice.
Yes, he kissed me once or twice.

After college Matt married Sally,
and they have always been happy.
I see them every five years or so,
and I always wear the bracelet.

This year my friend Ellie said,
Let me see that bracelet.
He gave it to you at Christmas?
He gave me the same one at Easter.
Then Sally said he gave her one too.
And also her roommate, Frances.
And perhaps some other girls,

for his eyes were green and his lashes curled up,
and he was tall with curly black hair.
I think he kissed me once or twice.
Yes, he kissed me once or twice.

Philomel, Postulant

I.
I stroke the dogwood's crippled trunk,
too bent to crucify;
reach up to nicked and scabbed blossoms
that slap against white light.

II.
I stand on the parapet
and Sister Procne unbraids my hair,
fans it out to the breeze,
winnows twigs, shakes scabs, scrapes burs.

Wind buffets twigs, scabs, burs,
lashes thrashes my hair,
whips the sisters,
wuthers their tower.

III.
Whispers—vats in basement,
Jewish babies,
twins, mothers
float in formaldehyde.

IV.
From the tower we all watch
me below in the meadow
on the plaid blanket
with the tall soldier,
eating grapes, green pearls,
the sunlight in my hair.

V.
My hair whispers, flutters above all trees.
They all play with my hair,
my sisters wrap strands around their wrists,
play peek-a-boo.
Leontine's a frog, Celia's a troll.

My pretty hair cascades over my shoulders.
They cup my breasts, I am so pretty.

VI.
He said he went down the basement stairs
of the German hospital,
saw in the concrete room
vats of Jewish babies, mothers,
black hair floating in formaldehyde.

Pear blossoms fall like snow,
cherry blossoms, confetti. Father.
My chocolate-brown hair,
so thick; he unwound it.

VII.
Soon they will cut it
they will laugh,
they will dance with it,
fling it to birds' nests.

How Long?

This morning I still feel your hands on my body—
they move across my back, down my sides.
How long will my skin remember?

I will not change the sheets yet.
I will wear the pale lace negligé.
How long will my skin remember?

I must wash your towel,
throw out your toothbrush.

I will bob my hair, lighten it to titian gold.
I will wear spike heels and miniskirts.
I will go to parties alone. I will flirt back.

I googled photos of boob jobs and tummy tucks,
considered the expense, the pain.
How long will my skin remember?

I do my sit-ups, work out at the gym every day.
I eat green salads and grilled salmon,
jog in Loose Park. My hipbones protrude.

I rub my hands over my body. My skin is soft.
You woke it up, you taught it to love back.
How long will my skin remember?

The Blue Neon Word

In a real bar, not a fern bar, a beer bar
with burgers eight ways to Jalapeño and Italiano,
back of the bar a blue neon script
Anglo-Saxon double four-letter barnyard word—
say it shout it sing it clap it stomp it
all the pickups picked up tight dance it—
word no old lady pearl-necklaced English teacher
high heeled—don't leer at me—can say
politely in a poem especially if she wants
NEA funding—stomp the NRA—
come on, Baby, leer at me,
just don't follow me
to the lady's room, phone booth, alley, my car.
Mamma said, *Even under baggy clothes
a man can tell your shape
so wear a good bra.*

Too Brilliant

Rushing toward me on the road is Jesus
in a burning bush, blazing, racing,
radiating, glorious: the sunlight glancing off
the fender of a silver motorcycle.

One car is a score of angels, fluffy white
and whirling, two cars, four cars proliferate,
transmogrify, transmute into waves of heavenly
hosts. The daytime sky flames cerulean,

deep but flat. As night falls the streetlights
start to rotate, radiate Fourth of July
sparkler halos. As the sky turns black the street-
lights catch fire, blaze out to whirling galaxies;

traffic lights explode red and green
and gold, and I am careening through a force
field of fireworks, and God and Trinity
and all their saints and angels and prophets are rushing

toward and around me, and God and everyone
who ever lived and entered into glory
are whirling around me, Jesus and Mary and all

my ancestors and every angel ever painted
by Fra Angelico or imagined by Dante
is whirling around me. And dark glasses do not help.

Portovenere

I. Last Night
I stroll the strand with George and Jane and Tara.
The sun has slipped into the bay, and silver
light is turning dark. Near on our left
a rocky island looms, then disappears.
Our steps slow down, our chatting stops, and here
a rough stone path leads up beyond the harbor.
Laughter, clapping, boats, and restaurant noises
rise, then die away.

The ramp fans wide and steep; we hear the sea
to right and left. Then all goes dark except
the stones beneath our feet. The sea breeze blows,
but I feel warm. Far up ahead, George takes
his jacket off, to cool himself, I think,
then holds it out before him like a shield.
I wonder. The girls walk in and out of light.

Spotlights assault us, the steps grow dark,
then vanish. Spotlights in our faces,
we walk blind, hold our hands up to our eyes,
my hands like praying, far in front of me.

We come upon the arched gate down to
the cave where Byron plunged into the Bay
of Lerici when he saw Trelawny snatch
drowned Shelley's heart out of the beachside pyre.
We see only boulders. *When* the cave
collapsed, we cannot tell. Iron bars, a sign
that cries *pericolo*, block the way.

We keep walking. It is warm. The spotlight
blinds us. We come upon a church,
people walking around it, talking softly.

Stairs to our right. The spotlight blinds me;
I hold my hands in front, then cannot grasp

the railing. Someone in front counting
one-two-three steps. People coming down.
I walk up into blinding light, stepping
into darkness. *Turn.* The light behind me
now. *One-two-three, turn. One-two.*

The ground stretches out—it may be flat.
The stones are uneven—it may be water.
May be nothing. Jane and Tara gone,
George up there somewhere. No stars, no light.

A tower blocks the spotlight now.
The stones are water, they fall away.
In arches to my right, couples nestle,
murmur. I hear Jane and Tara talk.
George speaks. They all laugh. I can't see them.

*The rampart, we are on the rampart. There
are the stars, the sea.* I lean far out, over
the rocks. Two stars float on the water, a few
lights out there somewhere. Where is the far
shore, what is it? The stars become constellations.
Jane says, *The stars on the water are smokers on the beach.*
The lovers in the arches hold their breath. We cannot
see or hear them. We do not forget they are there.

Jane says, *This is beautiful. We are in love.*
Who are we in love with? Who in love
with us? Jane is engaged, happy; George
is married, serious; I do not know about beautiful
Tara, the dancer, our *capitano.* These girls
are gazelles. I do not know about me. Am I
still, was I ever beautiful? Who loves,
will love me? I cannot transcend in solitude.

The lights to our left grow dim and disappear.
The rocks dissolve. The huge harbor promontory
pulls back. The constellations fade. Jane
and Tara do not see the fog; George
does not believe it is moving in. The battlements
shift, the lovers murmur. We turn from the sea
and the tower. The paving stones liquify. Tara
counts the steps. I reach out for someone's

hand, but all is watery darkness, and
the others go before—into the invisible
stairs, the spotlight blinding us—then
the stairs turn and the light is at our back.
The others stroll fast down the ramp, laughing.

I spread my fingers, join them far in front,
palms out, a shield against the light. I want
someone's hand, an arm around my waist,
to sit in an archway, to survey the cave of Byron,
now collapsed, to hear the seagull on
the rock cry out in a human voice. Lovers
nestle in the archways, and I walk on.

    II.This Afternoon
I climb back up to the ramparts in the late afternoon,
when the bay shines like a sequined swath as wide
as the world, as the sun assaults the waters and makes
them flare and burn like the face of God. The archways
are empty. Children, escaped from their mothers, scramble
up and down the rocks. The high platform
is solid and flat. I lean far out over
the rocks. There is no beach to stroll or smoke
or cuddle on. The lights I'd seen on the water
were markers for fishing lines. On Byron's rock
one man is sketching; another strips down and dives
into the sequined sea. A lady snaps photos.

In the little church of Saint Peter I light a candle,
pray that God will protect me from heartbreak.
A young lady in a gauzy white dress rushes in
from the sunlight, settles her dusty backpack on the bench,
kneels, hides her face in her hands, and sobs.
I step out onto the side lookout,
sheltered from sun and wind,
watch the yachts approach the harbor.

Millefiori

A Renaissance nun contemplates art

I. Triangle
A fat baby doll under the Christmas tree,
He gurgles, wriggles, twitches His toes. Mary
picks Him up, holds Him to her embroidered bodice,
and from its folds slides out her breast, guides
her nipple into His mouth. He rubs His face
against her breast, flutters His fingers. Now putti,
toddler Saint John and Joseph and Grandmother Anne,
shepherds and sages, cardinals and hermits and those
who paid for the paintings and all believers, doubters,
and curious stand by mother and infant—we dream
of our own loves, praise our Virgin protected
from pox and plague, we wash and powder and dress
all babies, kiss their chubby feet and hands.

II. S Curve
Jesus leans His head to one side,
hunches up His other shoulder, arches
His whole torso to lift up His lungs, bends
His knees to keep His feet on the wedged platform.
In every refectory, every monk's cell, above
every altar, I can slide my fingers
over lean muscles, smooth flesh, fevered, bleeding.
His head falls against one shoulder, His mouth
opens, His eyes focus on me. His eyes
roll back, His jaw tenses, His body writhes.
I bend, kneel, reach up, wail; the sky
blackens. He stares up, His face relaxes, He nods.
He gazes at me until I gaze back,
then He smiles the smile that only I can see.

III. Verticals

Holding the winding sheet, I lean the ladder
against the back of the cross, climb up, brace
myself over the arms of the cross so my hands
are free, and tie the cloth under the arms,
tightly. With the iron pliers I yank the nails
out of the wrists one by one and drop
them into John's uplifted hands. John
takes the pliers and pulls the nails out
of the feet, lifts them slowly off the wedge.
The body is too heavy, and I lower it slowly. No blood.
Still warm. John receives Him. I climb down
the ladder, help John lift Him onto Mary's
lap. I stand behind her, brace her shoulder,
hold His arm up, pose for Michelangelo.

IV. Triangle

As His mouth closes, He seems to smile.
He lies across her lap and she is young.
He is smooth and young, limp but lovely,
shining smooth. Her right fingers impress
His side, His wrist slides against her knee,
the satin folds of her dress caress his leg.
If they stood He would be just a little taller
than she, and they are young and there is
no flaw in them, behind their bulletproof glass.
And every day I caress, wash the bodies
of babies, the sick, the dead, my flesh longing
for Him in a dry and dusty land, and He
revives me in the midst of sharp arrows.

When a First Time?

It was late and we were tired,
so you just kissed me goodbye
in my hallway with all the lights still on—

but you held me for a moment
and we rocked back and forth—
and you ran your hands over my heavy wool coat,

and I felt the padding of your thick parka,
and under my coat I wore a heavy wool dress,
but I imagined you could feel my body,

though all you did feel was layers and layers
of scratchy fabric, and you muttered *Damn Winter*,
but we kissed enough to sway back and forth,

though it was late and we were tired
and you cursed *Damn Winter.*
And we have never even had a first time.

Except For

Except for the Rubens shapes,
you could say it was a midnight landscape
with art deco tree limbs
midnight blue and gray,
writhing Rubens shapes,
tendrils.

The blackbird sits on a lower limb,
then flies into the nest,
now crowded, hidden—
the leaves backlit,
the gray branches all vertical.

Now it is just we two,

though nine buxom musicians frolic
in the background,
Apollo piping,

but here with you all is elegant shade
curving limbs—

you wrap your soul around me
and keep me safe.

Black Glass Beads

for Sasha Bashkiroff

My evening purse, all black beads,
glistens like caviar.
Father gave it to me after Mother died.
Maybe he bought it for her
that summer in Petersburg.

Sasha my first love,
so strong, so handsome;
we fled across the steppes,
we caught the boat.

I need to be kissed,
dancing or kissing tonight—
but at least kissing.

I sew the purse back onto its metal frame.
The white-gray leather form shows
through the strands of black beading.
I cannot get them to close up
to cover the bone.
I walk bone on bone.

Mikhail will please please
take me dancing,
I will wear that dress
of gold and silver silk.

My Sasha settles in his chair,
plastic covers on the cushion,
newspapers spread thickly around;
he will sit quietly until I return.

I need to be kissed,
kissing or dancing—
my dress like silver and golden fire,
my purse like caviar.

Who was the tiny seamstress in
Moscow or Shanghai
who sewed this damask pattern
of ten thousand black glass beads?

Prunella

When Jason chopped the cherry tree
down, the one I loved
because Mother planted it for me
the summer that we moved

into this house, I asked him please
chop the tender branches
into little piles for me,
saw the trunk for stanchions

so I can make a little hut.
I hollowed out a Mom-
shaped bowl beside his tools and stuff—
after he gave me the space from

the back fence up to his shed.
My hut will mean when he's
away, that can be my bed,
a cocoon spun from debris

of grass and trash, my living igloo
in New Jersey. And when
it snows I'll pray to be a true
polar mother in my den,

back to North American
roots, so warm in the womb,
humming, sucking pemmican
snug as a bug in the room

of my own, my pink and blue squash blossom pendant—
Jason's gift to me,
a little faded from when I washed it—
hard against my cheek.

The Protectors

He squeezed blue soap
into a bucket of water,
turned on the motor.

Her face was calm.
I held her hand.

The motor droned.
I watched her face.
I squeezed her hand.

The motor surged
and all
the tides washed out
and out and out and out and out
and out to sea.

And the sea rolled on.

And she bit her lip
and her face went white
and I rubbed her hand and the tides
rushed out and out and

the motor stopped
and I heard
the tiny
sound
in her throat.

I Am Always Holding a Baby

a tiny new baby,
a little older than a newborn.
Always swaddled tightly
in a thin white receiving blanket
that pulls up over its head like a hood.
Its eyes are closed.
It never cries or squirms,
and it is not a doll.
It is warm, and I cradle it tightly
in my left arm, against my chest,

I need help.
I can take care of the baby,
but I need someone to open the door,
to drape my coat over my shoulder,
to pull out my chair,
to put my plate and my glass in front of me.

No one ever helps.
I am invisible.
My baby and I fade into mist.
Once, before I faded,
I tried to scold the other people
at the table;
they scowled at the sound of my voice,
and they looked right through me.

I need someone
to pull out my chair so I can sit down,
because, even though the baby is small,
my arm is getting tired,
and I am not strong enough
to pull my chair out with my foot.

Emily Is Sitting

Emily sits in a black marble bathroom;
she wears a long white dressing gown.
Her Love draws their bath, naked, perfect,
like young Zeus. They are in a hotel, or his home;

she does not know. She bites her lip to stay
alert, but slowly, slowly, she slides to the floor.
He turns, bends toward her.
She reaches out her hands, and he clasps them.
She whispers, *Jessica, her name is Jessica.*
Their child has quickened or died, she cannot tell.
She reaches toward him. She has forgotten his wife.

She reaches toward him.
She remembers she never married.
She rubs her hand across his satin back.

She remembers no children.
She caresses his beautiful face,
And it is her mother's embroidered pillowslip.

I Could Have Taken the Other Bridge

Traffic still flows onto the bridge.
Taillights linger far out over the river,
curve up the hill, candy necklaces, red snakes.
Frozen river—silver, gray—rejects
reflections.

Twenty miles per hour. Ten. Five.
I slide up to the white van. Stop.
Squeeze up. Texas plates. Scooch up tight.
Dust hieroglyphs its rusty doors.
Can't see over the top. A searchlight far
ahead. *Somewhere up there is an accident.*

The other lane moves forward,
cars too close for me to switch.
Someone's reading, someone's yelling,
praying. One may be flirting.

I'll memorize French verbs.
   Je t'aime
Sleet pocks my windshield.
   Tu m'aimes.
Wipers scrunch and scratch.
   Il m'aime.
Breath freezes.
   Elle l'aime.
Surely they'll clear the bridge.
   Nous vous aimons.
I've lost our dinner reservations.
   Vous l'aimez.
He'll be frantic.
   Ils l'aiment.
He'll leave.
   Elles l'aiment.

I memorize license plates.
Why didn't I take the other bridge?

Flashing lights.
Is someone sprawled on the highway?
Are they fitting a neckbrace?
Flashing lights.
Too dark to see any blood.

II

She Waits

. . . a woman, lovely in her bones.
—Theodore Roethke

When she rises from her perfumed bath, slender, gleaming,
and no one sees her, and no one *ever* sees her,
is she still Aphrodite? And why, at her age, does she still
need to be lovely? She has loved an older man
who hid her in this or that hotel while he dined
with this senator or that ambassador, and later
he would return, flushed and important, and order champagne,
and fall asleep soon. Now she pays for her own
hotel, waits perfumed, humming Mozart, for the sad young men
who want to love her, waits quietly in her room for their ring
or knock, the busy young men, too busy and worried
to arrive on time, to take her out, to notice
her efforts. His favorite perfume, the satin negligé,
the music soft. *Mozart disliked the flute*
but he wrote so beautifully for it.
If you tell her she looks pretty
today she will smile, and she will listen to your troubles
until she thinks she can trust you with a tiny one
of her own. Then she will tell you one part of a small
but important secret, and when you say *Not now*,
or say nothing at all, she will turn away. You will feel
her body tense. She will not breathe, and you
will realize she is trying to hide her tears. And when
she quivers, you will know it is too late.

Toronto

I.

All the air is lighted windows—bright
rectangles, parallelograms cantilevered,
floating, tunneling above the streets. I see
huge arches—not tendriled curving art nouveau
of 1890 Milano, but 1930
art deco—angled, stark, elegant
and huge. He stands tall and strong under
these vaults. We walk in the darkening city all
the sunless afternoon, feet light on concrete,
searching for some fort—we find the Union
Jack, discern, guess at, the fort beyond. With him
I am young. We walk three hours, nine miles, he says.

II.

The next three nights I dreamed of babies. X and I
were eating fruit in a Toronto piazza
that sunny October afternoon. He spread a
tablecloth, a brown and blue batik. I held our
fat baby on my lap; it snuggled against me
cooing. We chatted and laughed with our friends.
A street musician played. Leaves still clung to crisping
branches, the sky was gray-blue, golden air danced on
pale brick paving stones, glass buildings imprisoned us
in prisms, endless glass and leaves and laughter all
dancing babies and batiks in our golden air.

Then I was with my Irish grandmother folding
heirloom baby clothes, my pink tucked dresses, ribbonned
gray-blue capelets embroidered yellow, pink, and white;
father's linen romper suits; locks of golden hair.

Next, I had two babies—my delicate girl not
yet crawling, my robust boy ready to walk. I
held them facing forward, strolled through my golden rooms;
a garden party billowed into our house. I
paused before a grand gilt mirror. I smiled,

lilting. Someone snapped our picture. I seemed a
grandmother's age; were these my children? Grandchildren?
Somewhere was a young husband. Chandeliers sparkled.

    III.
Today I found a very old postcard, *Night view*
of Yonge Street, the cars as streaks of color, thick neon
tubes, tunnels of light; the air cold and dirty; newish
buildings, old-looking; a towered skyscraper lit
like a candle like a rocket. We must have walked
down this street. My knee then throbbed for six months.

You never called. When we met the next year
you said you had been so happy then that when
I left you were so depressed you could not call.

    IV.
Now I remember streaks of color, huge shop windows,
bleak lake air. Walking walking walking, you insisting,
The fort is just around the corner, it is just
over the bridge, the map says the bridge should be right
here, let's just walk over the highway, maybe it
is down this path. Dark and darker, no cars,
the wind died down. Where were the postcard's streaks
of light? Yes, the fort lay down that path, way down there,
under the bridge. But we turned around and walked back
for hours seeking the streams of light, and I was cold,
but you went off to swim for an hour. Never
said you liked my dress, almost fell asleep
at dinner. Never told me I was pretty.

    V.
Still, I say we sat in cafés,
you admired my legs, the sun shone,
we held a laughing baby,
the sun sparkled on the huge windows
prismed all around us.

Waiting All My Life

I.

Gold light slanted through summer leaves.
He kissed her beside her mouth,
and got out of the car.
She touched her face.
They could walk along the river, and
he could put his arm around her, and
she could lean her head on his shoulder.

My Love pounding into the earth,
Joyful joyful we adore Thee.
Stopped smoking, stopped drinking,
waited all my life,
your happiness means
oh please, so perfect,
Mine eyes have seen the glory.

Perfect diamonds, families' brunch,
two incomes, two incomes,
Whither thou goest.
Perfect dress, heirloom lace, Mother's veil,
china patterns, cookware, cooking lessons,
guest list, cruise deposit, plane tickets.

II.

—I can't sign this just yet.
—Just don't stiff me for the ring.

III.

She waters her plants,
digs around them with a fork,
puts her orchid on the windowsill,
walks on the Plaza at dawn,
and late in the evening.

She takes old magazines to Planned Parenthood,
old clothes to the Junior League Thrift Shop.

She cuts her hair, dyes it red.
Céline Dion sings, *When I fall
in love, it will be forever.*

Mothers ask *why*—
. . . right for each other.
She refused to learn to cook.
He was too intense.

Mothers tell her mother disaster stories—
He beat her after the wedding.
He beat her before the wedding and
*   her parents wouldn't let her cancel.*
He was gay, a woman, already married,
*   a fortune-hunter, deadbeat, playboy, drunk.*

Her face broke out.
Nonrefundable deposits.
Nonreturnable ring.

She heirloomed her dress.
She started lifting weights.
She bought hiking boots.

Mother Is Scrubbing Her Floors

Mother is scrubbing her floors, she won't use a mop;
she scours on her hands and her knees with a brush, says
she gets the corners, doesn't slop the baseboards,
says it's cooler down here, says it tightens her thighs.

Mother is polishing her silver and brass: she carries
baskets and trays of heavy objets d'art
down to the kitchen to soak in ammonia; with a toothbrush
she lathers her great-grandmother's cut crystal.
She climbs on ladders to wash Chinese vases.
She says it's aerobic, says Dad can take back the treadmill.

Mother is mending and washing and ironing;
she irons Dad's handkerchiefs, his shirts and his shorts.
On her knees beside the clawfoot bathtub she bathes
her great-grandmother's tablecloths, her napkins as large
as bridge cloths. With her rubber-gloved finger
she traces the monogram of Patrick O'Rourke;
she boasts, *One hundred years old*
and never been starched. Look: no tears, no holes.
Still so stiff they could stand up by themselves.

Mother strides from room to room opening
or closing the draperies, turning the lamps on
or off, watching the light dance on, caress
her furniture, her silver and brass and cut crystal.
She memorizes the contents of closets.
In a trance, she rhapsodizes
her ancestors' journeys to China and Egypt and Russia.

Who Will Hold Me?

Lines composed while listening to Aaron Copeland's
Latin American dances

I.
Who will hold me, onto whose large lap can I climb?
Who will enfold me, whose warm safe place can be mine?

Mary, the Mother of Jesus, can enfold me.
She rocked Him, sang to Him, she will surely hold me,
give me Christmas baubles tied with silk ribbons,
sing me to sleep in Heavenly Peace, with her children.
But no, she is too busy bestriding the globe,
stomping the python, perfect breasts exposed, adored.

Who will hold me, onto whose large lap can I climb?
Who will enfold me, whose warm safe place can be mine?

Jesus, my dear brother and Lord, can enfold me.
He comforted the sick, He surely will hold me,
school me in worship and Mediterranean
hyperbole, comfort me, lead me to heaven.
No, He is enthroned in gold
or walking dusty sandaled, preaching harshly,
or naked—flayed, and dying.

Who will hold me, onto whose large lap can I climb?
Who will enfold me, whose warm safe place can be mine?

God Almighty, Adored Father—He could enfold me.
Older than the hills now, surely He will hold me.
He is old enough to be a grandfather now;
His world He has created and punished for now.
He could lay aside His bronze thunderbolts today.
He could stop ruling and judging just for today.

Will He hold me, onto His large lap can I climb?
Will He enfold me, can His warm safe place be mine?

God Almighty, Adored Father, He will enfold me,
Give me brightly wrapped presents, read to me, sing to me.

He will sit on His grass, let me climb on His lap,
nestle up to His beard, soft and white as a lamb's.
If He let me stay, stroked my hair this afternoon,
I would not need a bright box with silk ribbons.

II.
When onto Grandfather God's large lap I climb,
and He enfolds me, His warm safe place becomes mine,

if I keep listening to these dancing flutes,
watching Copland's piano notes dance over
the hills, up and around the forests and mountains
of my Grandfather God, then I won't feel, remember

my father's hands on my throat, hear my Love
refuse to give me even a pretty box.
Just a bar of perfumed soap, just
a tiny something you picked out, pretty
ribbon and paper, I will save the box.

If I keep listening to these dancing flutes,
then I can't feel, remember

my Love answering, I don't respond to pressure. My kids
demand, and I give and give, and they complain,
are never satisfied. I hate I hate
presents. I will not give you a gift. I refuse.

If I keep listening to these dancing flutes,
with my Grandfather God, then I don't feel, remember.
He enfolds me, His warm safe place becomes mine.

Mother Mourns

Mother is mourning the end of summer.
She is saying goodbye to her white linen skirts.
She is saying goodbye to her pastel flowered sundresses.
She thought she could wear her dark cottons
just a few more times with a sweater or shawl.
She gave up bread and pasta and sugary tea all summer,
hoping to fit in to her tight white jeans by August.
And now in October she feels doomed and fat.

She refuses to zip up the garment bags,
to close the door to the storage closet,
to *entomb and forget.*
She hopes for more warm sunny days.
She says her new silk cream-colored pants
are *winter white*; she wants to remember to wear them
when that warm sunny day returns at Thanksgiving.

She refuses to turn on the furnace. *It's too soon.*
She sits in her cold dark house wrapped in a silk summer shawl.
The leaves turn gold and orange,
but she still yearns for pink and turquoise.
Halloween decorations cry out from the attic,
but she holds on to the forsythia wreath, to the lavender garland.

We need to bring the tropical plants inside.
She asks, *Isn't it going to be eighty degrees
over the weekend?* She plugs in the space heater
in the sun room and stares out the windows.

I try to remind her, *Remember how you hate the summer heat?
Remember your dozen cashmere sweaters in jewel tones?
The sparkly St. John knit you got at the store closing?
Your shoes and tights and big gold jewelry?
Haven't you missed them all summer?*

She says, *Eight months until I see my white linen skirts again.
Will they fit me? Will I live until then?
The summer flew by, and I didn't even wear all my clothes.*

Portuguese Motets

Tallis Scholars, Cathedral of the Immaculate Conception, 8 March 2008

Beside the altar, the large wooden cross, draped in purple.
Jesus, larger than life, shining, sculpted of burnished silver.
So thin, every rib protruding, his head bowed,
his heavy loincloth knotted and draped.
So thin, so sad. Not yet transcending.

The choir sings
all her beauty has departed from the daughter of Sion.
Their voices sweet and high
stir a secret part of my soul,

and I feel your lips on my throat and the side of my face.
I lean back against you, and you lift up my hair
and kiss the back of my neck, and I lean back against you,
and you run your hands over my heavy fur coat,
and I imagine your hands on my breasts,

and the choir sings
of all the precious things
the daughter of Sion possessed in ancient times . . .

and I fear your promises and predictions.
I fear your huge and airy house,
your hands on my flesh.

The choir sings
Father I have sinned against heaven and before you,

and I am afraid of your huge house
and your hands on my imperfect body,

and the choir sings
Blessed are the dead who die in the Lord,

and I will buy new silk garments and put garlands in my hair,

and the choir sings
O God our savior be merciful to our sins for your name's sake.

I fear your promises to care for me,
and your predictions that I will come
to your house and you will care for me,

and the choir sings
Lord I have no one to lead me into the pool
when the waters are disturbed.

I do not clap,
I do not want to jar the music in my body,
I want to keep the thrumming deep inside of me.

And beside the altar hangs Jesus,
His cross draped in purple,
his corpus silver,
so thin, every rib protruding,
his head bowed,
so thin, so sad—
does He want me to accept the invitation,
is it He who sent the temptation—
what does He ask of me?

Mother Remembers Flowers

Not flowers, really. She never planted anything in her life.
She thinks flowers come in a long box tied with a silk ribbon,
or else prearranged in a lavender crystal vase.
She would be horrified were I to inform her that
in order to have a flower garden
she would need to get down on her knees
and dig in the dirt.

What Mother remembers are corsages.
She says she received a lot of them
and always pressed them in a great big book,
until the spine broke, and she had to find another book.

She said it was the family Bible.
Now I know this is not true
because she grew up Catholic,
and they never had a family Bible.
She has a tiny gold-edged green leather Bible by her bed,
but I can tell she has never opened it.

Still, she remembers her corsages.
She says that she received so many that
once a week she set aside time to care for them.
She unwrapped the narrow ribbons,
peeled off the green tape, pulled out the green wires,
and smashed the blooms as flat as she could
onto a paper towel with the heel of her hand.
Then she found a page in the Bible with a nice illustration;
in pencil at the top of the page she noted
the name of the boy and the date and the occasion.
Then she laid the smashed flower on the illustration,
closed the book firmly and sat on it for a few minutes.

The nice ribbons she saved for her hair;
the ordinary ones she rolled up and hid in her top drawer.
She inserted the pearl-headed pins into her
great aunt's embroidered pincushion.
She still has the pins, and there are a lot of them.
But I have never found a single dried flower
in any book, large or small.

To the Virgin in Saint-Sulpice

I.

Swathed in marble, she holds her baby aloft,
bestrides the earth, crushes the serpent,
the firmament radiates from her. Waves swell
over the globe, billow around the columns,
down to the altar, around the bronze crucifix.
She is Venus being born, a bacchante dancing.
I will light a candle to her.

Steam rises from my bucket, soapy water
drains from my mop, I scour these stones, glistening,
my body thick as a tree, my skirts swirling.
Lady Goddess, mother of stars and hills, you are
almost as old as God, young as a tree.

The bishop consecrated me a virgin,
the pope decreed that I am humble and small,
worthy to serve. I kneel to burnish these stones,
my brush stiff inside my sopping black rag,
my hands rosy with soap, fresh smelling.
My legs are sturdy; my skirts ripple and slosh.

II.

Lady Godddess, mother of the hills, larger
than God your baby, satin waters churn
around your legs, you march through marble waves,
stone drapery armors your soft parts, you
are my age, no shaft or sword can penetrate us,
mountains unsurmountable bigger than Venus,
stronger than bacchante and wood nymph, not for seducing,

not for touching, but for bestowing. You
show no fear or hesitation; your hair and robes
whip the winds, churn the waters, command
the firmament. Before the universe is, you are,
with God, of God, you beget God's Son, hold Him

up high; clouds purl out, surge about you
and sweep into the sea that rumbles down

and around the twisting columns, and you crush the python
that flails out behind your feet, the sea serpent
that writhes, its mouth open, and you have dominion
over winds, rain, sea. Priest, bishop,
pope can roar, can dictate my actions, but I never
need a man to tell me what to think.
Your Babe will grow, be crucified and stabbed,
but always you saunter the waves, Help
of Travelers, Tower of Ivory, my Mother, Sister.
Sun Moonlight Sea Planets: hail
to Thee oh Queen of Light. Arc of the Covenant,
Star of the Sea, the Empyreum calls thee Mother.
I light candles to thee and I am free.

Veni Creator

Sufficient unto the day
the evil thereof
      when you cry to me,
      since we can't marry.

Sufficient unto the day
the joys thereof.
      Ice melts in rapids,
      country snow, slick hills.

Sufficient unto the day
the evil thereof.
      Stars light the abbey,
      bells toll at midnight.

Sufficient unto the day
the joys thereof.
      Monks sing at dawn,
      boys' choir—all angels.

Sufficient unto the day
the evil thereof.
      The priest knew my name,
      Jesus touched my hand.

Sufficient unto the day
the joys thereof.
      Altar wine's tart-sweet,
      enough for today.

Daddy Said

Your mother was so pretty—
her cheeks flushed, her eyes got dark
when she was mad.
I liked it when she cried,
then I could comfort her.
I was her Hero.

Your mother was so pretty,
a stream flowing bright and dark,
deep, churning mad.
As hidden rivers cried
to the sea, one day her
soul sought its Hero.

Her cheeks flushed, her eyes got dark,
she ran in mad
circles as eagles cried,
called her name, asking her,
Who is your Hero?
They told her she was pretty.

When she was mad,
eagles and rivers cried,
echoed, tried to find her
home, name her Hero,
for she did not feel pretty
when sun, moon, and stars were dark.

I liked it when she cried,
I wanted to save her,
to be her Hero,
to teach her she was pretty—
soft, gentle—not forest-dark,
moon-circling mad.

Then I could comfort her,
become her Hero,
give her a house, a pretty
talking bird, cut her long dark
nails, stop her mad
summer solstice songs, cries.

I was her Hero,
the one who called her *pretty.*
She was afraid of the dark,
not really mad.
Eagles, planets, sea cried
to her; we all loved her.

Black Jack

Our family has no new stories now that my father, Black Jack, is dead. An old girlfriend with red hair called him that because when he had it, his hair was black. Black Irish with bright blue eyes, like his mother Mollie O'Rourke Cleary, who still had dark curling hair at ninety. Moorish, Spanish, who knows? Daddy was Missouri, just a generation removed from Ireland, quite jolly and loud. He was an only child. Mother was the oldest of five. Daddy liked having a lot of in-laws. He thought they liked him too.

He always said he liked *to stir things up.* Mainly he liked to aggravate Mother. Helen Elizabeth Kelton, sedate New England Episcopalian. Her family liked to sit quietly and ponder.

Daddy liked to hear Mother scream, *Jack, Jack,* as he took the hairpin turns along the cliffs on Trail Ridge Road or raced speeding trains across Kansas. But mostly he liked to give large parties. With scant preparation.

PICNICS

I

Mother came out into the side yard with a pristine platter of deviled eggs and the Italian bowl of her famous unreplicatable potato salad. She was wearing the crisp navy-striped sundress that she had just finished sewing. I was carrying the two red-flowered linen tablecloths that I had just ironed. (Mother disliked ironing so she delegated that chore to me.) We were heading to the two picnic tables that Daddy had crafted from scratch and had just dragged out from the kitchen and the screened-in porch. Mother was expecting about a dozen neighbors for a midsummer picnic.

About two dozen people of all ages were in the yard. More people were streaming in through the front and side gates. Every man held a beer bottle, every lady wore a fresh sundress and a big flowered hat and little white sandals.

Daddy was standing on a step ladder by one of the dining room windows, removing the screen. Before Mother could make a sound he bounded over to a flaming hole just that size and flung down the screen. Then he started grabbing handfuls of ground beef from a cookie sheet and dropping them, quickly-formed, onto the screen.

Daddy asked a man in a navy blazer to go to the store to get thirty pounds of hamburger and buns and pickles and mustard. He handed a shovel to another man and told him to dig another hole in the lawn. Daddy dashed over to the other dining room window to get its screen. Someone dumped coals into the new hole, grabbed the sports pages from an old lady in a rocking chair. Squirted lighter fluid, tossed in lighted matches, *foomsh*. Screen, more wobbly hamburger patties. *Hey Ed, run to the store and get more meat, beer.* People started singing.

Mother did not dare to scream. She set the table. Porch furniture and blankets appeared on the grass. The whole Democratic Party. Irish whiskey and beer.

Children were climbing the jungle gym, swinging on the swings, jumping and laughing at badminton and croquet.

I don't remember Mother raising her voice. She did go inside for a moment. I think she was smoking on the screened-in porch on the other side of the house. Unfiltered Chesterfields. A splash of Chanel N°5, a little bug spray. Fresh lipstick. Back outside she smiled and nodded and smoked with the ladies she knew. She had done all she could.

II

Black Jack was so pleased with what he considered the success of his home picnics that he tried his same technique for a garden party on Mother's brother, my Uncle Stanton. At Uncle Stanton's country estate. That's what it was. Bucks County, Pennsylvania, George Washington-era stone and clapboard house, rolling lawns and fields, swimming pool, gardens carefully tended though not manicured, an historic graveyard, horse trails through old-growth forests. Uncle Stanton, gentleman farmer and chemist, rode to the hounds and chaired historical museums.

Once Daddy dug a barbeque hole in Uncle Stanton's lawn, near the slope down to the swimming pool. Three dozen relatives from four generations, basking and chatting and swimming. Daddy must have thought he was being helpful, joining in. Uncle Stanton must have been horrified. I was not there. I never heard of it until last year. My cousins all loved Jack; they all came to his funeral.

Sailing

Daddy flew in the Army Air Corps in the Pacific Theatre, but when he settled down in landlocked Kansas City after the war he took up sailing. A little lake was being built in Wyandotte County, and then another one in rural Jackson County. Daddy needed a sailboat. Basements in those days were just basements, with cracked cement floors, a drain in the middle, crusty cobwebbed windows at eye level, a bare lightbulb hanging from a ceiling crisscrossed with pipes. And ingress and egress—wobbly wooden stairs down from the kitchen, and an outside exit up crumbling cement steps through those old double *Wizard of Oz* tornado doors.

Here, in the evenings after Mother had taken down the sheets and diapers festooned on crisscrossing clotheslines all over the basement, Daddy would set to building his sailboat. He built three dinghies over a few years. First the twelve-foot Tern, then the sixteen-foot Y-Flyer. After he could not extract the Y-Flyer through the *Wizard of Oz* doors and had to disassemble it inside and then reassemble it outside, he built the twenty-foot Flying Dutchman outside entirely. I remember snow on the tarp because he could not get it finished before winter. He formulated and cooked his own glue, he mixed his epoxy and laid on his chopped-strand mats of fiberglass. He sanded and polished the wood trim. The Flying Dutchman's mast was two fine planks of Sitka spruce. Each inch of each successive sailboat he sculpted finely, lovingly.

He cut and sewed and grommeted his own sails. Wise enough not to purloin Mother's ancient Singer, he bought his own industrial sewing machine. He laid the fabric out on plywood tables in the unfurnished parlor of a cranky neighbor. His thoughtfulness did not extend to the drying of the precious sails. Arriving home too late for dinner on Sunday evenings, he would drape the sails on the Queen Anne dining-room table and across the Chippendale chairs.

Daddy was enthusiastic and creative but alone in the family. Mother and Cathy and I liked the picnics by the lake and chatting with other families. I have films of the fall picnics—the ladies in plaid skirts and blazers, the men in bomber jackets and felt hats. Mother did not sail—by then there were two toddlers to tend to. But Daddy tried to teach Cathy and me to sail. Our only interests were sunbathing on the deck and deliberately capsizing the boat so we could cool off. We never could understand angles of the wind and *coming about* and *hard-to-lee*.

Mother Won't Wear Walking Shoes

He had patterns that had been cut through
like the windows of Saint Paul's in either shoe.
—Chaucer, "The Miller's Tale"

Mother won't wear walking shoes.
Her topaz and ruby heels spike
in gratings, shred on brick sidewalks.
I show her Bally flats, Adidas;
she says, *Henry won't love me*
shod like that.
Her calves are matchsticks.
I point to wheelchairs.
She says, *I tuck under,*
my legs are steel.
She silicones amethyst suede platforms,
disdains my L.L.Bean boat shoes.
Her boots, laced high,
have patterns cut through like cathedral windows.
She says, *Henry told me,*
"Don't buy shoes without me."
I say, *He's in London*.
She says, *He'll know.*
He's buying me slippers
to sip champagne from.

Mother Won't Buy Polypropylene

Mother was invited skiing.
I tell her about polypropylene.
She calls it polygamy-ethylene-acetylene.
I give her a fuzzy blue ear band,
loan her my black hood.
She complains, *I'll look like a terrorist.*
I send her out for a parka.
You can't ski in mink, I explain.
What would Catherine Deneuve wear? she wonders.
She insists the geese in my down coat are dead.
She comes back with a yellow cashmere sweater.
On sale it cost about the same as polyethylene, she reasons.
Those Tibetan goats are still alive, she argues.
I send her out for jerseys and long johns.
She comes back with a gold jacket.
I'm old enough for gold lamé.
I ask, *Where will you wear it?*
She resolves, *It brightens up my apartment.*
I might ask some people over.
I can wear it to the movies.

Elva Remembered

The Daughter Remembers
Perhaps Elva had been abused.
Perhaps she felt poor.
Perhaps she was jealous of Mother—
her lovely children, the big house.

She told me that Mother did not love me.
She said that everyone hated Mother.
Elva was the only one who loved me.

She read to me. She sang to me.
She held me in her arms during my nap.
I was in school all day, but I am sure
she held me while I slept.
She rocked me. She was there every day.

Elva bought me flowered dresses.
She signed Grandpoppi's name to checks
and shopped at Swanson's. She dressed me in pink lace.
Mother got ugly Sears-catalogue polyester.

Elva held me tightly while I slept.
No one will ever love me like that.
I was traumatized when she left. I was six.
I will never find a love like that.

The Mother Cries Out
I just found out what Elva did to my child.
Forty years ago.
It is too late to kill her.
I am sorry that she is dead, because I would do it.
I did not know what she did to my child forty years ago.
My daughter just told me—she just remembered.
It is too late to kill Elva.
It is too late to protect my child.

The Daughter Reveals
We lived with Grandpoppi.
Mother and Daddy slept late on Saturday mornings.
Sister and Brother and I climbed into Grandpoppi's big bed.
He read to us.
He hid candy for us in his bookcases.

My room was across the hall.
The bedroom doors were partly closed.
I peeked out.
I saw the priests and Mother and Father
in Grandpoppi's room for a long time.
I saw the men with the stretcher on wheels
take him into the hall and down the stairs.
I looked out the window—
they wheeled him out through the garden gate.

Elva told me that when Grandpoppi died
Aunt and Uncle would throw Mother out in the street,
and Elva would have me all to herself.

But when Grandpoppi died Elva left.
I never saw her again.
Daddy said they did not have as much money.

I went to school all day.
Mother said I did not need a nap.
She bought me new furniture: a canopy bed,
sewed flowered curtains.
But she did not buy me fancy clothes.
She did not give me candy.
I wore a uniform.
Mother let my hair grow long, curled it with a curling iron.
She did not hold me while I slept,
she did not touch me under my clothes.
She sat on my bed beside me all night when I was sick,

but she never looked at me without my nightgown.
I knew she did not love me.

    The Mother Clamors
Does this explain things?
The low-cut dresses, micro miniskirts—
in eighth grade?
The smoky eyelids and bright lipstick?

The pot and vodka?
The bus-stop pick-ups?
Hurried trips past hecklers?
Sudden marriages and divorces?
Does this explain it?

    The Daughter Entreats
It was always the same man, just different faces,
always Elva I needed, searched for.
No one ever touched me inside like she did;
she hurt me, she loved me.

    The Mother Appeals
What do we do now?
She has remembered.
She has talked.
She has prayed.
She is a good mother.
No one is hurting her now.
What must we do?

Mother Is Dying

for Sarah Curran

Her doctor says my mother is dying.
Mother is, my mother is dying,
dying. He says, *Your mother is dying.*

She is beautifully groomed and bejewelled.
She has not told us. Every day she dresses
and puts on her makeup and sits in her chair.

She has not told us—my mother is dying.
Mother is Mother is cancer floating
beautifully groomed dying beautifully

in blue gown, blue mother-of-the-bride
blue satin, blue lace—floating in blue
negligé, sitting swathed in warmed

satin quilts, Mother is talking,
not telling, not letting—her hands resting,
long white fingers, blue jewels, blue veins

so-white hands, picking her blue quilt's
silk binding, talking, not letting—
chasing me down in her car. I race

through pine trees, she's stalking me down
through some field to the edge of some
winter-covered swimming pool, I slip

under the icy blue cover, trip—
down steep concrete stairs into my
blue world, swirling blue, speeding speeding

bullet dolphin speeding to crash
of shouts clapping gold trophy trophies
shouts clapping and my mother has
        cancer cancer cancer is dying.

For Yvette Chauviré (1917-2016)

And the mother's beauty is ministering motherhood,
and in the old woman there is a great remembering.
—Rilke

The old ballerina has created her face
out of Loves she has had or imagined,
out of Loves she has held or lost.
The old ballerina has created her body
to sway and to quiver like a swan,
to tick and to tock like a doll like a clock,
to run mad through the forest.

In street shoes before the mirror
she shows the young dancer the mood—
Keep the elbow low. Your arm is a wave—
a drop of water runs down from your shoulder,
rolls down along this curve,
rolls down the length of your arm,
drops down, drops down, drops down, drops down.

The young dancer's arms are stiff.
You reach out to your prince.
The ballerina runs her hands along the girl's arms,
bends and straightens her own fingers,
strokes caresses the girl's hand till
she bends and straightens her own fingers,
reaches out to her prince.

The ballerina holds the girl's waist,
presses her fingertips against
the girl's spine, her flanks.
The two ballerinas glide across the mirror,
they reach their arms up, back.

You pass the gates of hell.
You are on an empty plain.
You are in a dark woods.
You don't see your lover.
Your hands reach for the vacant heavens,

your hands crash behind your head,
your elbows point to the absent heavens,
your fists clench behind your raised shoulders.

Yvette pushes the new ballerina to the music,
twirls her, spins her off
as a mother first suckles her infant,
then lets it walk run grow long blond braids,
watches her grow long blond curls, round breasts,
seek love in the forest.

Chinese Box of Love Scenes

I told Edith that Maurice dreams of me
with a young man. I hate that. Edith told me
about another Frenchman she saw. On a
Paris metro car a young country man
pushed past her, plopped on the pop-up seat by the door.
A violinist was playing Mozart's Alleluia.
Through a gap in his brown teeth the peasant whistled
at the beggar, scratched his own curly hair,
gnawed a greasy finger. He drooped
his thick shoulders and closed his eyes.

At the Concorde Metro stop a woman
clearly in her mysterious years got on,
poised her greyhound body languidly
against the pole. Edith studied her
for inspiration: tight jeans,
tuxedo collar on purple silk jacket,
straight blond hair.

The country man rubbed his face with crusty
knuckles, popped his eyes open, then jerked
his head back as if two weights were falling
inside his skull. He swallowed hard as if
he had dry bread in his mouth. He ran his eyes
down the woman's satin lapels, across
her tanned décolletage. He stared at her soft
face, turned to see what she was looking at.
She watched the map above the door,
the darkened windows, nothing.

He sat straight up. Edith nodded at him,
smiled, but his eyes were caressing the woman's hair,
her bare earlobes, her neck. At each stop
she closed her fingers on the pole. Her nails
were long and oval, Schiaparelli pink.
At each stop his eyes kissed her from

fingertip to wrist. At Louvre, Edith
noticed a plaster Diane de Gabies, her fawns
beside her, in a lighted niche. The woman
looked at the goddess, smoothed her own hair.
Her jacket still revealed no more than
the diminishing V from throat to waist.
At Bastille the young man stood to get off,
blue eyes sparkling at her. She moved out
of his way but never looked at him.
He got off the train and turned to watch her.
The doors closed, and he kept on staring.
She never saw him. His face shone.

Edith says had I seen that young man
I might know why Maurice still speaks
so reverently of his first Love,
who was fifty when he was twenty or so.
I might know why he wants to find me
a young lover. I may be
his woman of mysterious years.

But he is my apple tree among the trees of the wood,
a sachet of myrrh lying between my breasts.
And my belly is a heap of wheat set about with lilies,
my breasts are two fawns. He feeds me with raisin cakes.

After Reading about Chinese Foot-binding

My feet freeze under the quilt—
it is too heavy, my instep cramps up.
Stabbing pain on my instep as if broken.
Toes arch back, curl against the soles;
the cramp thickens, slides up my leg.

My feet are cold. I cannot sleep.
I hold them in my hands, but they do not warm.
I need my lover to hold them,
only he can warm them.
They do not ever warm.
The cramp on my instep is a thick rope,
my toes draw up, fold under.
I hold my feet in my hands, rub up and down,
all along the cramp.
They do not get warm, they do not unbend.

I dream of Chinese lotus feet,
soaked in hot water and herbs, animal blood,
the bindings soaked so they shrink as they dry,
feet wrapped every day in hot cloth
soaked in animal blood, herbs.
Pull the bindings tighter, they shrink as they dry;
the arch cracks, the toes break,
force them under, flatten them against the soles.
Necrotic flesh peels off,
toes can break and fall off.

Caress my perfumed feet,
thrust them into your mouth,
my curled lotus leaves, my tiny feet.
I embroider many silk slippers.
I cannot walk, I cannot sleep.

The Bride

I glanced from the hallway
and saw her emerge
from her perfumed bath
to stand dripping
under the skylight,
glowing like Aphrodite,
rubbing gardenia lotion on her belly,
eating a peach.
My daughter,
a little pregnant,
still foam-covered.

I see Cytherea, motherless,
begotten glowing perfect
from the sacred foam
of dead Ouranos's immortal flesh.
Surrounded by swimming putti,
by Tritons blowing conch shells,
she emerges on her scallop shell,
all gleaming and peach-luscious.

My daughter, well-mothered,
soon to be fluffed in white lace,
veiled in hope, his Aphrodite.

My Burberry Raincoat

I.

I strolled into the shop—
and all the sales associates wore brilliant tight black,
extreme spike heels for the ladies,
rock-star jeans for the men.

My outfit was old and frumpy and too colorful,
and really really passé, an English plaid
a schoolgirl would have worn forty years ago,
and in fact I did, a skirt very like this one.
This one was only twenty years old,
from Brooks Brothers, a big leap upgrade
from my homemade high-school uniform—
fine for my real life but definitely not chic enough
for this trendy shop. But when I walked in
they liked my red beret and welcomed me.

James, a music conservatory graduate,
a pianist and composer of operas,
showed me the classic raincoat,
designed by Thomas Burberrry
a hundred years ago for the trench officers,
suggested I get the smaller size—
it fit my shoulders, it would fit over my suit jacket.
I wandered around while he ordered the wool liner
from San Francisco, and I found a darling hat to match
for more than I had expected to pay for the coat.

I bought it all. None of it on sale. Never on sale.
I do not need it. Not for warmth, not for rain, not for style.
I cannot justify it. It cost as much as a good used car.
It cost as much as a trip to the beach.
All my friends are at the beach.

James folds the coat into thirds lengthwise, then by width,
forms a perfect envelope of itself.
He wraps it in two layers of black tissue paper,

secures the paper with a chic black seal,
inserts the coat into an ivory-colored bag
embossed with a jousting knight in shining silver armour,
lance thrust out, horse at full gallop.
James snips off the black satin ribbon at a perfect diagonal,
threads the ribbon through and back across
the top of the bag and ties it in a Christmas bow.
My coat, my perfect coat. My sunny afternoon.

    II.
I should have bought this coat years ago.
But then I did not have the money.
Then I did not need it.
Then I still had hopes for a young lover.
Now I still do not need this coat. But I have it.
I love it. I may sleep with it.

But it does not help.
It does not bring him back.
He is in hospital, or he is in Algiers,
or he is with her. He is not here.
He is not coming back.
He will never even see this coat.

With him I saw the face of God—
the world was in balance.
No one ever held me like that—
not parents or husband or lovers.
With him I felt whole.
With him I learned to trust.
With him I did trust. For a while.
And then that terrible phone call,
and I got so ill I ended up in hospital.

It is too late for me.
My skin wrinkles while I am not watching,
Nothing sags, but everything is withered.
It is too late for Botox or a chemical peel,
too late to be seen only by ivory candlelight,
too late for love.

III.
Nanette, don't mess with me.
You may be at the beach,
you may be able to travel with your husband
and go out to dinner and dancing,
and you may have a lot of coats like this,
but now I have one too.

The next time I go to a bar with my friends,
no young guys will try to pick me up
by saying I remind them of their grandmother.
I am not their grandmother,
I am English royalty—they all wear this coat.

IV.
Why doesn't it rain?
Why is the weather so warm?
I can't just prance around in this coat
to the grocery store or the doctor's office.
Why doesn't it rain? Why doesn't it get cold?

Remembering the good times—
does that bring them back?
Does that make today sadder?

Menaced by Flowers

(the paintings of Frances Cohen Gillespie)

Poison-color cattleya orchids
loop Laocöon-snakes, octopi
lariats, around me as I sneak
away; tentacles twirl out in front,
sway back, to attach my face.
Fanfold velvet mouths open,
pulsate, ruffle, in static breeze:
silk secret-flesh—engorged, enflamed.
Steel leaves, stems, banana petals—
billow, sway, roll, without moving,
without air water earth, without
sound, noisily. Sylphs, ondines, gnomes—
stifled—hide, dissolve. Salamanders
—dry, frozen—rule. Mirrors undulate,
brocades furl, surge. Flesh
makes its own calligraphy.

Irises in the Tribal Grill

The day of our first date was damp and windy.
Behind you on the ledge, a dozen buds,
their sepals still enclosed, their sword-leaves still
adhering to their stalks, leggy, stuck.
Cobalt and cerulean blues, with bright
and dusty sunlit yellow eyes. The vase,
a heavy prism, caught the light and danced
it back onto your face and hair. I made
you turn around and look, then we forgot
to talk. Doubled in the window-glass,
the irises—through that glass, an infant,
hooded in his baby seat, his face
shadowed by flowers, smiling at the lights.

Lace

(After seeing the Treasures of the Czars in Topeka, Kansas)

The last time you loved me, this is what I saw:
leaves piled up gold and orange in diapered patterns,
with deep brown shadows, their edges licked silver
by the sunlight, still and moving, blowing
into the hair of the Sidhe, hardening
like the faces in a Neptune fountain,
water flowing from his mouth and into
the folds of his cheeks, his hair, and lacing
into the shapes of ancient keys to Kremlin
gates: Saviour, Secret, Borovitskii,
Trinity, Saint Nicolas, all on crimson
velvet cushions; golden domes, all the
earth's uncut jewels in jungle colors
exploding around and in us fast and slowly
the pink sky edged in blue, the hand of God.

Katherine Dunham: on Haitian Dance

You use the floor as the earth.
You pound your feet upon her belly,
and her force flows up into you.
You slap your feet upon the earth,
knees bending, body writhing.

Your pelvis is center.
Holding torso and legs together,
you work for fluidity,
moving like a goddess,
undulating like water, like the ocean.

Knees bending, body writhing,
you slap your feet upon the earth,
her force flows up into you,
and you are ocean and earth, you catch fire.

One Single Blueberry

He asks for a hamburger,
he eats only one fourth of it;
still, that is much more
than he has eaten in all of two weeks.

He drinks some coke, he swallows with pleasure,
but he coughs.
He drinks some more, and he smiles.

He says that he feels well, that he has no pain.
He smiles at me,
he says that he likes my dress, my hair.
He says that it was very wise
of him to marry me.

    How long will it suffice—
    a taste of meat, a few drops of coke, of water?
    He is getting thinner, he has nor muscles nor flesh.
    Nothing but his bones.

He takes a piece of orange,
big as the tip of my finger.
He asks for more fruit.
He takes one single blueberry,
he sucks on it, smiling.

He refuses to eat his cookie.
He refuses to take his pills.

His voice hoarse, one can hardly hear him.
He asks to see some old friends—
Georgette, his first wife,
whom he married when he was only six
and she was only three; two other childhood pals.

Une Seule Myrtille

Il demande un hamburger,
il n'en mange qu'un quart;
quand même, c'est beaucoup plus
qu'il a mangé en tout depuis deux semaines.

Il boit du coca, il avale avec plaisir
mais il tousse.
Il boit encore et il sourit.

Il dit qu'il se sent bien, qu'il n'a pas de douleur.
Il me sourit,
il dit qu'il aime ma robe, mes cheveux.
Il dit que c'était très sage
de sa part de m'épouser.

    Combien de temps est-ce que ça suffirait—
    un morceau de viande, quelques gouttes de coca, d'eau?
    Il maigrit, il n'a ni muscles ni chair,
    Rien que ses os.

Il prend un morceau d'orange,
grand comme le bout de mon doigt.
Il demande encore du fruit.
Il prend une seule myrtille,
il la suce en souriant.

Il refuse de manger son biscuit.
Il refuse de prendre ses pilules,

La voix rauque, on l'entend à peine:
il demande de voir des anciens amis—
Georgette, sa première femme,
qu'il a épousée quand il n'avait que six ans,
et elle en avait trois; deux autres copains de jeunesse.

I ask him if I should telephone his cousin Thomas
with whom he had a dispute ten years ago.
He responds, *No. No, he was trouble.*
Thus I know that he is still alive.

> When will it no longer suffice,
> the sight of our faces,
> a few drops of water,
> one single blueberry?

His nurses recommend hospice.
They say it no longer suffices—
a few drops of water, a single blueberry.

Je lui demande s'il veut que je téléphone à son cousin Thomas,
avec lequel il s'est disputé il y a dix ans.
Il répond, *Non. Non, il créait toujours des problèmes.*
Comme ça je sais qu'il est encore en vie.

    Quand est-ce que ça ne suffirait plus,
    la vue de nos visages,
    quelque gouttes d'eau,
    une seule myrtille?

Ses infirmières proposent l'hospice.
Elles constatent que cela ne suffit plus—
quelques gouttes d'eau, une seule myrtille.

The Alarm Clock

Frederick said, *I need an alarm clock for travel.*
Helen checked Macy's and Halls;
ordered a treasure from Cartier.
Frederick smiled, *That's nice. Thanks.*
Bought your Christmas gift on the plane from London.
They wouldn't wrap it. What you asked for.
Helen kept the Chanel Nº5 in her purse, close.

When he was next in town, for four days,
Frederick picked her up at work.
Two hours late, the fourth day.
So busy: barber, real estate deal, car polished.
She pushed her index fingernail into her thumb.
I'm sad we couldn't get together yesterday.

He said, *Look, I told you. Doing my best.*
She bit her knuckle, *I understand; I'm just sad.*
He snarled, *If you're going to be like this I'm sorry I saw you at all.*
Helen's throat clenched—like swallowing calcium pills without water.
She stared at the parquet floor, at the chandelier.

He said, *We've got an hour. I'm being picked up for the plane at seven.*
He said, *Great time last week in Paris: Embassy, Opera.*
You would have loved . . . Best performance I ever . . .
She asked, *How was my clock?*

Great, perfect.
I exchanged it for the lapis and gold one.
Always wanted. Only three hundred more. I paid the difference.
Will always remind me of you.

Helen moistened her lace handkerchief
with Chanel Nº5, daubed at her wrists.

Only His Bones Remain

A cruel man is dying.
His stockbroker is visiting.
The ambulance waits in the driveway.
The cruel man is choking.
He aspirates.

Fluid fills his lungs, his fever spikes.
MRSA invades. Sepsis rages.
His heart thumps. His blood pressure drops.

In hospital he gets morphine,
oxygen, antibiotics, a feeding tube.
His body withers, only his bones remain.
And his staring eyes, his rasping voice.

> This is what I want for him:
> I want him to cry out like Gounod,
> *Oh Lord take pity on my distress,*
> *Do not reject my sinful soul.*
> *De profundis clamavi ad te, Domine,*
> *Oh Lord, hear my prayer.*

> I do not need for him to admit that he betrayed me.
> I do not need to confront him.
> I do not need him to plead for my forgiveness.

The nurses chat quietly in the hallway.
The nurses laugh gently in the hallway.
The rain falls softly in the courtyard.

Lightning spikes through the windows,
vengeful justice shakes the windows.
The cruel man enters into eternal life.

When Sylvia Heard Her Orpheus Singing

It was the God in you I wanted to touch the God in me.

My birthday. How old am I?
We sat in the car for a while.
The rain started up again, but softly.
We sat in the car for a while and talked.
He kissed me beside my mouth.
My birthday. How old am I?

We could walk along the river,
but he is so young.
I could put my head on his shoulder.
But he is so young.

America: The Concerts

I. BACH MASS IN B MINOR

Kyrie

Breathing, up and down. Breathing.
Surely God will have mercy.
It is not a sin to want,
to feel the music gather.
Is it a sin to want,
to feel the music gather
in the small of my back,
to fan out along my limbs?
Is it a sin to spin through the petals
of the ceiling rosettes, wheeling?
Oh, would he turn and smile,
would he just look at me?
Would he turn and smile,
would we walk along the river?
He is so young. How young is he?
How young am I young?

He will not look at me,
he regrets his kiss beside my mouth
in the rain last night, our kiss in the rain.

He knows what could happen—
what would happen if we walked toward the river?
If we walked toward the river, what could happen?
Because it is not raining.

    Gratias agimus
I could thank God, thank God
that my body is honey in sunlight—
Thank God that I could lie
in the grass beside the river,
rose petals, redbud petals blowing over me,
and he would worship my beauty
and I would rise to meet him.
Please, God, let me not be too old
to feel. Yes, I feel, I am not too old to feel.
I am too old. I am wise. Yes, wise,
wise enough not to do. Yes, I see us by the river,
yes, I create my memories, I imagine my joy.

    Domine Deus Rex Coelestis
Soprano, tenor, flute, blend
like spring breezes,
redbud and rose petals,
dogwood, magnolia, on my skin
by the river in the grass.
Oh do not touch him
or lean toward him
or glance at him—
we do not have the right,
but, oh God, thank You for the thought,
my mind by the river in the grass.

II. DEBUSSY, PETITE SUITE FOR PIANO FOUR HANDS

Today I'll watch each moment one by one.
He'll kiss me one slow kiss at a time
all over my face and neck and shoulders

for a long time until I am fainting.
Promise me, oh Lord,
that every time I hear a violin or piano
I will feel him kissing me slowly,
slowly, caressing my hair.
Promise me, oh Lord, each moment one by one,
each melody, from each violin and piano.

III. STRAVINSKY'S PSALM

Lente lente currite noctis equi.
Slowly slowly may ye run, oh horses of the night.
The horns transported us,
the myriad flutes and oboes and cellos,
oboes crescendoed, flutes and cellos,
violins crescendoed.

They stop. They all stop.
The psalm abrupts,
the horses of our night ran, they ran on,
they ran swiftly swiftly away.

Italy: The Air

I. MILANO

Duomo
We climb the spiral staircase
breathing smoothly, no fatigue.
He holds my hand as we scale
the very acme and pitch of the roof,
edge our soles onto the flat stones
shining blue-gray, silver-white in the mist;
he stands close beside me
as we look over the balustrade,
survey the city, the sculptures,

and talk, talk slowly.
He teaches me about Milano, its artists;
about mental equipoise, sophrosyne—
giving each thing its proper time and care.
The air is warm and moist,
the city silvery blue in the rain.

    Sforza Castle, a Last Pietà of Michelangelo
I never liked Him, you know. He was too wild—
yelling at moneychangers, preaching that stuff,
rude to His mother, aloof and strange.
But then I came around the corner in the Sforza Castle
and there He was, His legs beautiful and polished,
His lovely body so thin, His mother leaning over Him unsculpted.
Why am I so moved by this last Pietà of Michelangelo?

II. The Lido at Sestri Levante

Iridescent water-bubbles
pump out from a tube on a cylinder,
larger and larger, they wobble and waver,
heavy, too heavy; they break free, divide,
float up past the children and horses
going slowly around and around on the carousel.

III. *Childe Harold,* Canto IV, Venice section

    We inhale the ambrosial aspect
In the Camogli train station,
the *Super Rapido* speeds by.
Across from the tracks, in an arched wall,
bright purple wisteria blooms profusely.
Wearing a grass-green shirt and white pants,
our *professore* reads to us.
The pages shake and ruffle,
a crowd stands and listens,
all smiling quietly.
We inhale the ambrosial aspect.

IV. ABOVE PORTOFINO

Descending the hills with feet pointed sideways
like Fred Astaire, and then dancing,
then exhausted with walking high in the heat,
and then coming upon the baroque church.

V. FRIDAY 19 JUNE, I THINK

Time has stopped. We walk and walk and walk
and then look back at the sea and at the hills
we have just climbed, smell the flowers,
sit on a rock in the shade, drink water from our bottles,
keep walking walking walking up steep stone steps,
and then over rocks and larger rocks,
and boulders that never were or will be steps.
At first, there are houses, corn, and bamboo,
walls with morning glories and bougainvillea,
window boxes with geraniums, garden gates.
We see tennis courts sheltered from the sea
by cypress trees and a Roman arched wall.
People going up and down with baskets, wearing sandals,
a man carrying a new door with a large glass window in it.
We turn onto a paved road and walk along
to a little restaurant where we stop
on a walkway covered with vines.
We walk and walk and then there are no houses,
no shade for a long time, then finally into woods
with dappled light, now I can keep up,
and I am at the front of the slow group.
We come to the top of the hill and see
the other side of the bay and look down on the Cinque Terre.
Lunch at the abandoned and ruined Augustinian
hermitage of Sant'Antonio, a lookout for Saracen raiders.
One hates to think of this land threatened, at war.

In the distance, the towns hum,
even on the mountains we hear some distant machine,

but when we sit still there is only chirping and breathing
and the low murmur of our *professore*
reading Shelley or Byron.
Tara silently applies a wet bandanna to my neck.
My breathing slows, my tears dry on my face.
Our *professore*'s voice goes on, the breeze ruffles the grass.
Far below are terra cotta towns, ochre and madder,
with green shutters, palm and cypress.
Behind us are groves and vineyards.
The sea is out there somewhere.
Ahead and all around, only glare and dust.

VI. SATURDAY

As I walked on the Lido I reflected and pondered
and finally stopped and stared into the bay—
at the lights along the train route and by the tunnels,
lights on the gelati stands on the beach,
and in the restaurants, and on the small boats out in the bay,
and the few lights sparkling on the hills,
Everyone doing the *passeggiata*,
a very different rhythm than in Milan,
where everyone wears black and white and strolls deliberately,
each person at the same pace.
Here ladies wear white wedge sandals
and yellow print and blue flowered dresses,
the children dance, and all the houses are brightly painted.
I was solitary and alone and sad,
not really missing anyone, needing and wanting to be alone.
I had wanted to dance, but I knew why I was not asked.
My vicarious pleasure was very gentle.

What could be, what might be, what is.
I am glad I know your hands, your mouth,
the touch of your skin, so that when
you are walking with the group I can remember
and not just imagine ignorantly.

I could never have imagined.
It is as if you were an angel sent to encourage me,
to heal my soul. A gentleman, an angel of grace.

When I think of you I smell the flowering trees
along the path to the funicular.
I stop to smell the gardenias.
You go on, but I catch up.
I smell the oleander and jasmine.
We walk on in an easy quiet, our group behind us.
They do not know my thoughts
or why I am smelling the flowers.

When we come back down, you have the map,
but we take a different route,
and I do not find the gardenias.

VII. SUNDAY

The only place free at the breakfast table
is beside you. Everyone looks dreamy,
perhaps from last night's *limoncello*,
or the morning's clear air.
I sit down next to you, next to you.
Without reflecting, I say,
I had the most wonderful dreams.
Your breath jolts.

I will remember the air
that touches my skin so I cannot feel it.
It is air the way it should feel,
so we never shudder or start or cringe—
our sweat cools us,
and always the air is sweet on our skin.

If I ran my finger along your arm,
if I could kiss your mouth as he read to us,
if I could walk into my room

and you would follow me
and we could look out this window together—
yes, it is easier that I know your skin is golden,
that I have heard you speak to me alone,
that you have told me of your sorrows.
Oh do not let that last time be the last time.
I dreamed I reached into my purse and pulled
out a bottle of champagne, chilled, and two goblets.

The Slut of Now flickers between Anticipation and Memory.
I will withdraw to shed the skin you withdrew from.

Patricia Cleary Miller is professor emerita of English at Rockhurst University, where she founded and edited the *Rockhurst Review*. She is the author of *Starting a Swan Dive* (Daniel L. Brenner Award) from BkMk Press, as well as the poetry titles *Dresden* and *Crimson Lights*, and the nonfiction title *Westport: Missouri's Port of Many Returns*. Her work has appeared in *Stand, Connecticut Review, New Letters, Cottonwood, I-70 Review*, and elsewhere.

Her secondary school was the French Convent of Notre Dame de Sion. She is a graduate of Radcliffe College (where she also held a Bunting fellowship), the University of Missouri-Kansas City, and the University of Kansas. For eight years she was poet laureate of the Harvard Alumni Association. She is a past president of the Writers Place and won its annual Muse Award.